Table of Cont

Introduction [illegible]
Chapter 1: Ready for the Stock Market! 7
How Does the Stock Market Work? 9
What Are the Most Common Ways of Investing in the Stock Market? 11
How Can You Make Money Investing in the Stock Market? 16
Understanding the Different Types of Stocks 18
Overview and Introduction of the Various Investment Opportunities Within Stocks 20
Traditional Investment Advisors 21
Robo-Advisors 22
Online Brokers 23
Different Types of Trading 24
Stock Market Terminologies 29
Chapter 2: Using a Ledger to Track Your Progress 32
What Is a Ledger? 35
What Goes Into a Ledger? 36
How to Make the Most of Your Ledger 38
The Importance of Keeping a Personal Ledger 40
Everything Your Ledger is Going to Help You Track 42
Everything You Need to Know About How to Fill Out a Ledger 45
Best Practices and Knowledge for Evaluating Investment Performance 47
Portfolio Standard Deviation 50
Recording Scenarios 54
Chapter 3: Establishing the Best Investment and Trading Strategies for You 58
Different Types of Investing Strategies 59
Types of Stock Investment Opportunities and Their Respective Benefits 63

Best Stocks to Invest in and Why........69
Avenues of Portfolio Management and Their Respective Benefits........73
Understanding Basic Trading Strategies........75
Chapter 4: Expanding Your Investment Knowledge and Network........79
The Importance of Building and Expanding Your Network........80
How to Build Your Network........83
The Importance of Expanding Your Investment Knowledge........86
The Basics of Stock Trading........88
Strategies to Expand Your Investment Portfolio and Make Steady Profits........93
The Importance of LLCs for Investors........97
How to Set Up Your Investment Company........100
Marketing Strategies for Your Brand........109
The Best Investments for Passive Income........114
Chapter 6: Personal Investment Ledger........117
Benefits of Keeping an Investment Ledger........118
Chapter 7: Money Management Tips........121
Conclusion........126
References........132

Stock Trading Ledger

The Secret to Successful Investing

Alan Newton

Introduction

You might be familiar with this famous quote by one of the most successful investors of all time, Warren Buffett: "wide diversification is only required when investors do not understand what they are doing". How would you interpret Buffett's opinion on diversification?

For some, this is their cue to withdraw from all other investments and put their resources into the one they believe to be the strongest. The problem here is that not even Warren Buffett uses this strategy. It is one that leaves the investor extremely vulnerable. It presumes that there is a way to accurately predict the future. There isn't. So long as we have to operate in volatile and uncertain economies, diversification will always be the golden rule of investment.

So, was Buffet wrong? In fact, he was spot on. He simply meant that diversification should not be used as a way to mask utter ignorance about how to properly invest. When you are ill-informed or have no real knowledge about investing, you could fall into the trap of widely diversifying your portfolio.

Diversification isn't the only band-aid used by some investors to cover up their bullet wound of ignorance. For some, it is faith in their vast supply of cash that can enable them to survive after numerous mistakes, or paying other people to make investment decisions for them.

In the end, nothing beats knowing what you and your money are getting into when it comes to investing. If you have decided to create a stream of passive income by investing, you must begin this journey by gaining useful knowledge in the particular sectors that you have chosen. And this is where this book, ***Stock Trading Ledger***, comes in.

The merit of this book isn't only that it has been written with simplicity, such that even those who have no idea what stock trading is can be enlightened and edified by it. ***Stock Trading Ledger*** has also taken into consideration many of the pain points expressed by new and experienced investors.

One common problem is the issue of networking. While you may not choose to set up a Limited Liability Company (LLC) for your investments, you will still need the help of other successful and experienced investors to find good deals and make profitable decisions. But what are the steps to go about expanding your network? And what is the right attitude to present in the world of investment?

Successfully growing your network of investors isn't the only issue that is tackled here. What if you do want to set up a company for your investments? First, is this even the right move? But more importantly, how would you go about this unusual venture?

It's not enough to get the right paperwork that qualifies your company as an LLC. In fact, for example, you might find that trying to register your business with the Securities and Exchange Commission (SEC) and Investment Advisor Registration Depository (IARD) is the easiest part of establishing your company. Once that is finalized, you must think about branding, delegation of certain tasks (hiring), and marketing. These three—branding, hiring, and marketing—are some of the biggest reasons why new businesses fail. This book will strip down these concepts and provide time-tested solutions.

By reading ***Stock Trading Ledger***, you will learn the various paths that investors can take into the stock market. You could buy and sell stocks, which is the most common option for traders, or you could invest in bonds, mutual funds, index funds, and exchange-traded funds (ETFs). If you have always sought a comprehensive explanation for these trading options, you will find them in this book.

Maybe you're not exactly a fan of stock trading. Instead, you can give the real estate market, hedge funds, or commodities a go. Although this book focuses on the stock market, you will learn just why investing (whichever way you choose to do so) is the key to financial security. As such, you should find some way to grow your money by investing.

This largest portion of this book is dedicated to stock trading journals or ledgers. In fact, two separate chapters in this book discuss the subject: one is concerned with the understanding of ledgers, while the other allows the reader to actively record their trading experiences. This is because the only way to grow as a stock trader is with a journal. Now, your journal doesn't have to be similar in every way to those of other investors. But it should help you remember the past and reveal both your flaws and progress.

Probably the biggest problem, especially for new investors, is the scarcity of correct and comprehensive information on how to invest. There is no shortage of internet gurus selling courses and sure-fire strategies. This is not to say that there aren't honest and experienced stock traders sharing their wealth of knowledge, but they are uncommon and often they are catering to those who already know the basics of investing.

This book caters to everyone, regardless of their level of knowledge of stock trading or any other investment. You will learn about ledgers, and the difference they can make in your journey as an investor. You will also learn how to discern the best investments and the best strategies. Do you want to connect with other investors and enrich yourself from the veritable pool of knowledge? Then you need to find out how to build your investor network in Chapter 4 of this book.

Maybe you have held back from investing your money because of the very real fear that something could go wrong. After all, investments with zero risks are just myths. They have never existed and, most likely, never will. However, even if you choose to found your own startup and invest in the growth of your business, there is always the risk of having all your effort, money, and dreams go to waste. As such, whether you are a venture capitalist or stock trader, chances are that you could be wrong about an investment and lose all your money. Do not let this fact scare you away from investing, but do not invest blindly and hope for the best. You can figure out how to mitigate the risks and make sure that you are not completely defeated.

At the end of this book is an entire chapter dedicated to financial management tips. Even if you were wrong about a trade and lost money, you can remain in the game.

Now, you might be wondering what qualifies me to make these assertions and promises. You might agree that there should be no higher qualifications regarding the stock market than the financial success that the investor has achieved and the time they have spent in this industry. On both measures, I can boldly say that I've passed glowingly.

I'm presently in my mid-thirties, but I made my first investment in the stock market when I was 20 years old. In the past decade, I've managed to grow my investments to the point where I now earn between six and seven figures every month. I've been able to achieve a life of ease and luxury—my dream life. I can travel wherever I want and whenever I please. Isn't this the kind of life that many people hope for? I know it was for me.

At this point, I should make it clear that I do invest in the stock market merely because I'm hoping to make a quick buck. The internet is rife with get-rich-quick approaches to stock trading. But very few, if any, work. It is dangerous to try to make money in any industry when your only motivation is greed. You have to love or at least be excited by the industry that you're in. This is what pushes you to keep learning, keeps you grounded when challenges come, and helps you grow. And I *do* love stock trading.

I have loved it since I made my first investment a decade ago. I learn and apply new strategies to generate profit. Over the years I've even developed a few of my own. I understand the risks that come with stock trading, but I'm excited by experimenting with various methods to mitigate those risks and grow my portfolio. Although I invested for the first time when I was 20 years old, my interest in the stock market (and investing in general) began years before that.

This book is important to me because I believe that everyone can achieve the same results as I have, if they know what I know. In my opinion, it would be quite sinister to hoard all the knowledge that I've garnered through the years. Today's world is marked by increasing poverty and unstable economies in many countries. For those who are interested in stock trading, I would much rather that they do not make the same mistakes that I did in the beginning. I'm also passionate about making sure that people do not fall prey to scammers and gurus who are only out to make a quick buck, and do not care about the effectiveness of the information that they disseminate.

In this book, I will share with you the steps that I took to achieve financial freedom. Earning six figures for the first time is not enough. You also need to know how to organize your funds and use your money to produce even more. This is a skill that I have learned through decades of trial and error, but you can gain in a few minutes of reading this book.

Putting this book together is not my first attempt at teaching other people what I've learned about money and investing. I've watched many of my friends grow financially by listening to and implementing my advice. While this brings me immeasurable amounts of joy, I hope that this book will help a much larger population of stock traders and investors become successful.

Investing remains the single most consistent way to build wealth. When you think of the richest people in the world, you might assume that their only source of income is the business that they are known for. For instance, it's easy to believe that Mark Zuckerberg only makes money through Facebook, Instagram, and other related ventures. While his business decisions in these social media applications account for the larger percentage of his net worth, Zuckerberg has also been known to splurge on various real estate properties. Elon Musk, although already a millionaire, recognized the potential of Bitcoin and invested $1.5 billion into the crypto currency. In fact, Elon Musk's business history is marked by numerous investments, from X.com (which later became PayPal) to Bitcoin.

If you are still unconvinced about the importance of investing and learning how to do it right, consider this: even though we tend to dissociate our present selves from our future selves as two different entities, it is actually prudent to make sure that 30 years from now, you'll still enjoy financial security. You should invest as a part of your retirement plan. Indeed, what part you play in the stock market and how you manage your finances to multiply them can be what determines whether you will enjoy a relaxed and happy future or one that is filled with regret.

Again, this book uses everyday words to explain and comprehensively demystify investing. One of the biggest turn-offs for new investors are the unfamiliar words and complex mathematical and financial concepts of the stock trading and investment world. No, you won't need a business administration or accounting degree to wrap your head around the information and solutions in this book. If, for instance, you've always wondered what ETFs, mutual funds, individual funds, and brokers are, and have never really gotten a satisfying answer, you are going to put these questions to rest by reading this book. ***Stock Trading Ledger*** is your key to finally unlocking the secrets of the most successful investors ever!

Chapter 1: Ready for the Stock Market!

The stock market is a public exchange system created to trade and issue stocks that are listed and traded over-the-counter (OTC) or on exchanges. Stocks, otherwise regarded as equities, are fractional partnerships of a company that are listed on the stock market for investors to trade ownership of their investible inventories. When the stock market works efficiently, it can improve the economic growth of a region. This effect is because companies can easily obtain public-sourced capital through stocks. The term stock market can also be used to describe some of the key players (indexes) in the market, such as the S&P 500 or the Dow Jones Industrial Average. This is because the market comprises several different stocks, making it impossible to keep up with all of them. However, the main indexes help to narrow down range, as they involve every area of the stock market. Thus, their performance in the market can be used as a general representation of the performance of the market as a whole.

So, next time you turn on the TV and see a headline describing a swing in the stock market, the gist is typically about the movement of indexes up or down in the market. This implies that such indexes have either appreciated or depreciated in value over the course of a trading day. Investors make profit by trading on the movement of stock prices. In another sense, the stock market is a collection of several exchanges and markets where trading and issuance of shares listed by publicly held enterprises are conducted. For such financial activities to occur, institutionalized OTC marketplaces and formal exchanges must operate within the confines of certain regulations. A particular region of the country may field several different stock trading venues for transacting stocks and other kinds of equities.

Stock exchange is a common term used interchangeably with stock market, but both are distinct in and of themselves. Stock exchange is a subset of the stock market. Simply put, if you trade in the stock market, it means that you obtain and offer equities or shares on one or several other stock exchanges, which make up the general stock market. In the United States, some of the leading stock exchanges are the Chicago Board Options Exchange (CBOE), the New York Stock Exchange (NYSE), and Nasdaq. These pioneering national exchanges, together with other smaller or larger exchanges operating within the country, make up the United States stock market. Although the name implies that stocks or equities are the primary trade of the stock market, that really isn't the case. The stock market trades a variety of financial securities such as bonds, currencies, commodities, derivatives and corporate bonds based on stocks, and exchange-traded funds (ETFs).

How Does the Stock Market Work?

From the previous discussion, we deduced that the stock market is an umbrella housing a network of exchanges on which companies list shares. In turn, investors are open to trading these equities amongst themselves based on the movement of stock prices. The bulk of investors on the stock market are big-time funds that control large amounts of money, but individuals are also allowed to trade stocks through brokers, such as Acorns. However, this doesn't describe the entire process of the stock market.

You might have come across TV scenes of buyers and sellers trying to trade stocks at the New York Stock Exchange. While the stock market used to be a physical marketplace during the early years, like the American Stock Exchange and the New York Stock Exchange, nowadays financial securities are traded via a network of trading platforms. That is, transactions are now performed digitally and not physically. Another noteworthy process is how stocks are managed. While most stocks are listed on exchanges, public listing isn't a compulsory feature for trading stocks. This is where over-the-counter markets and private stocks come in.

Perhaps the most important part of how the stock market works is determining share prices. The price of shares on the stock market is determined in several ways, but the typical process is done via auctions, where buyers and sellers make offers and bids to trade securities. Bids are the prices investors make to purchase equities, while offers (otherwise known as asks) are the set prices of equities. When bids and asks match, trades are made. The general stock market comprises millions of traders and investors, each with unique ideas and perspectives about the value of any given stock, which influences the prices at which they intend to sell or buy securities. The many different transactions happening regularly as traders and investors put their intentions into action by selling and buying stocks results in the minute-by-minute changes in the market through the course of a trading day.

The stock market creates a platform for such trades to be carried out by matching sellers to buyers. For an average investor to access a stock exchange, he or she requires a stockbroker. Stockbrokers are the middlemen between buyers and sellers. To get a stockbroker is as easy as creating an account with any well-established retail broker in your area.

What Are the Most Common Ways of Investing in the Stock Market?

- **Stocks**: Otherwise known as equities or shares, stocks are the most common type of financial securities and the simplest investment in the stock market. When buying a stock, you are purchasing a percentage of ownership in a publicly traded enterprise. Most of the largest companies around the world are publicly traded, such as Facebook, Afterpay, General Motors, and Apple.

- **Exchange-Traded Funds (ETFs):** ETFs share similarities to mutual funds because they are both collections of investments used to track a certain market index. However, unlike mutual funds that are obtained via a fund company, the shares of exchange-traded funds can be sold and bought on the stock market like regular securities. Additionally, ETFs undergo fluctuations in prices over the course of a trading day, whereas the value of mutual funds is determined by the net asset value of an investment and is calculated after every trading session.

- **Bonds**: When buying bonds, you are indirectly lending money to an enterprise. Usually, the enterprise is government owned or managed by a business. Municipal bonds are issued by local governments, while corporate bonds come from companies. Some examples of bonds are bills, notes, and Treasury bonds, and are issued by the United States Treasury to investors as debt instruments. During the duration of the bonds, the lender receives payments of interest. At the end of a contractually agreed period, or when the bond matures, the lender receives their principal.

- **Certificates of Deposit**: Certificates of deposits (CDs) are investments with low risks. Here, you give banks a certain amount for an agreed period, after which you receive your principal and a predetermined interest. Interests vary according to loan period, with longer timeframes attracting the most interests.

- **Mutual Funds**: Mutual funds refer to financial pools created by multiple investors to be invested in several different enterprises. They can be managed actively or passively. For the former, a fund manager is required to choose the securities for investing in mutual funds. Typically, fund managers attempt to overcome a given market index by picking investments predicted to outperform the said index. Passively managed mutual funds, otherwise known as index funds, are quite the opposite and rely on tracking key stock market indexes such as the S&P 500 or the Dow Jones Industrial Average.

- **Options**: Options are one of the more sophisticated securities on the stock market. Think of them as a complex method of purchasing stocks. When buying options, you are obtaining the permission to trade an asset at a given price at a set time. Options are classified into two types: put options (for selling options) and call options (for buying assets). The risks associated with options is that the value of stocks tend to dwindle. Otherwise, should there be a dip in the initial value of the stock, the investment is lost. Options represent an advanced technique of stock market investments that should only be indulged with caution and careful calculations.

- **Retirement plans**: Retirement plans aren't necessarily a distinct type of investment in their own right. Instead, they are conveyors for making investments, such as purchasing funds, bonds, and stocks, which exempt the investor from taxes. This tax exemption comes in two forms: withdrawing money without having to pay income tax or investing pre-taxed monies (as in traditional IRAs). The risks associated with retirement plans are no different from those linked to investing without retirement plans.

- **Cash**: Cash deposits at the bank are one of the easiest, safest, simplest, and most comprehensible investment assets. Not only are investors aware of the exact interests their money garners over time, but they are also shielded from loss because their capital is guaranteed. On the flip side, interests earned from cash deposits stuck in savings accounts seldom ever overcome inflation.

- **Commodities**: Commodities refer to physical products that are available for investing on the stock market. They are widespread in futures markets that bring commercial buyers and producers together for the purpose of hedging financial stakes in everyday commodities. Before investing in commodities, it's imperative to completely understand futures, which is necessary for investment because of the risk that the price of commodities could suddenly move in any direction based on real-life events. For instance, the price of oil could spike or dip due to the political statement of the government of a region.

- **Hedge Funds and Private Equity Funds**: Hedge funds are investments made on a variety of assets with the goal of achieving above market returns, known as alpha. However, the performance of this investment isn't guaranteed, as hedge funds are prone to drastic shifts in returns and may underperform the market by a huge difference. Typically, hedge and private equity funds are only available to certain accredited investors, as these securities require large sums of a million dollars or more for the initial investment. There is also the tendency of features such as net worth requirements that may be imposed on these funds. Both types of investments could hold down the capital of investors for long periods.

- **Cryptocurrencies**: Cryptocurrencies refer to digital currencies that are unbacked by governments or traditional finance. They can be traded via cryptocurrency exchanges or bought and sold peer-to-peer (P2P) with retailers. Cryptos are one of the riskiest forms of investments as they tend to experience wild market fluctuations.

- **Real estate**: Investors can purchase real estate directly by obtaining residential or commercial properties. On the other hand, they can buy shares in real estate investment trusts (REITs). REITs serve as mutual funds in which a group of investors pool resources to obtain properties. Real estate is traded like stocks on the stock market.

- **Annuities**: For many, annuities are vehicles used in part for retirement savings plans. In buying an annuity, you have successfully obtained an insurance policy, for which you are entitled to certain periodic dividends. There are several forms of annuities based on the policies offered by traders.

Some could last an entire lifetime, while others could span an agreed timeframe. Additionally, premium payments could be periodic or a one-time upfront payment. Annuities may be linked to the stock market partially, or have no direct affiliations to the market, existing as mere insurance policies. Also, payments could be immediate or stalled until a certain time. Annuities can also be variable or fixed, based on how they are traded.

It's possible that you feel somewhat overwhelmed by the terms listed above. That's quite natural, especially if you hadn't previously given much thought to investing. Before you get to the end of this book, however, you will have become more familiar with these terms.

How Can You Make Money Investing in the Stock Market?

Before you delve into trading the stock market, understanding how to make money from purchasing financial securities is a necessary requirement. While the process might seem complex on the surface, it's relatively easy at its core. There are three main ways to economically benefit from investing in stocks:

- Receiving cash dividends
- Sharing in the proportional growth of the underlying earnings on each share owned
- Receiving more or less per $1 profit made by an enterprise based on the general level of optimism (greed) or panic (fear) in the economy at any time, which doubles the valuation multiple. This process is also known as the price-to-earnings ratio.

For certain businesses, the first method of profit sharing, dividend yield, is a substantial business method. For others, sharing cash dividends is not feasible because all of the returns gained by the business are generated from the second method of profit sharing, growth in intrinsic value for every fully diluted share. For example, in more than 25 years, the software giant Microsoft has grown to billions of dollars in valuation of its net income per year. The third component, the valuation multiple, is in a constant state of fluctuation, though throughout the company's history it has successfully averaged 15 times its

earnings in the United States. Simply put, throughout history, the market has been willing and capable of paying $15 per $1 of net profit generated by a business.

Understanding the Different Types of Stocks

There are different ways to invest in the stock market. They each present varying degrees of risk and reward, and it's up to you to find which type of stock fits your goals and risk tolerance.

Range Bound Shares

These types of stocks are ones that don't experience any overwhelming dip or spike in price, with variety typically bordering within a -5% range. The enterprises that enlist these stocks tend to encounter stagnation in profit growth, meaning the enterprises are stable at their core and have no substantial thrust into profits.

Range bound shares are one of most common stocks traded on a technical basis. They are utilized by participants who sell them off at the higher end of the product range and are acquired by investors willing to purchase at the reduced end of the product range. At the end of the day, investors stand to gain a reasonable profit margin of 5% (or more, depending on the agreement) per five days or more.

Blue Chip Stocks

These stocks are listed by enterprises with firm roots and years (decades or even centuries) of records. The companies aren't necessarily high development companies but are capable of providing investors with stable returns on investments. Blue chip stocks have a better and more reliable spending and results history than their counterparts.

For instance, the Dow Jones Industrial Average comprises the bulk of these stocks. Blue chip companies experience stable but reduced development and are relatively one of the safest places to invest and store money. What's more, they offer amazing compound annual returns across multiple years.

Speculative Stocks

These stocks belong to enterprises with little to no fundamental ideology. Hence, the principles of their stock deviates from conventional logic. The stock prices listed by such companies tend to spike and dip multiple times across a single trading session. The reason for such volatility stems from the fact that stock prices are affected by the information mill and can be easily manipulated by selling and buying at the Telstra Corporation Ltd (TLS) share price instead of the fundamentals. Fundamental analysis is the difference between using technical analysis to observe the historical price of a stock and measuring its intrinsic and fair market value.

Speculative stocks are the riskiest types of stocks and one of fastest methods of losing money. By all means, avoid these stocks.

Growth Stocks

Growth companies are at an all-time high. The enterprises behind these stocks experience increased rates to share prices, as well as business turnover. These businesses occupy areas of the economy that are constantly in the buzz, hence their attention is almost unavoidable.

In the basic sense, growth companies haven't been around for as long as blue chip companies. However, their stocks tend to be pricier in comparison, varying with the stability of enterprises. In contrast, growth stocks are somewhat prone to significant spikes and dips in share prices in a handful of dealing classes because of the large trade interests involved. Additionally, due to never-ending attention, stock prices could fall significantly with any negative news involving the listing organization. However, you can mitigate this by choosing growth stocks in industries that enjoy mostly positive buzz.

Overview and Introduction of the Various Investment Opportunities Within Stocks

There are different types of stock investment platforms. Which one you decide to use will depend on how you want to invest, and what involvement you want to have in the decision-making process.

Traditional Investment Advisors

The stock market still has multiple investment management professionals dedicated to working with investors on a personal basis. These professionals help with portfolio management, particularly after determining the risk tolerance, time horizon, and investment goals of investors. They go on to create portfolios consisting of several common investment opportunities in the market, such as individual stocks, mutual funds, and ETFs, among others considered appropriate for an investor's profile.

For new investors, the chances of being involved with traditional investment advisors is limited. These professionals tend to handle investors with large portfolios measuring as much as $500,000 and above, although some may descend as low as $250,000. Keep in mind that traditional investment advisors tend to command relatively high management fees per annum, which may range between one to two percent of the entire value of an investor's portfolio.

Additionally, the sale and acquisition of bonds and stocks may attract some form of trading commissions, as well as load fees demanded for some mutual funds. A good example of traditional investment advisors is The Paladin Registry, which is a directory of financial planners (fee only), who recommend financial advisors to clients based on their areas of residence.

Robo-Advisors

Robo-advisors have only been in the market for about a decade now, but they have since bloomed into a popular choice for investors. The reason for such widespread acclaim is not farfetched; they perform the services of traditional investment advisors, but at a much cheaper and affordable rate. For instance, a robo-advisor typically charges between 0.25% to 0.50% of the entire value of an investor's portfolio as annual advisory fee. Additionally, they don't demand trading commissions, because they don't invest in individual stocks, and there are no loading fees because they steer clear of mutual funds. Robo-advisors also assess investor profiles in the same way as traditional investment advisors. To begin, the investor fills out a questionnaire with which the system determines the personal risk tolerance, investment goals, and investment time horizon. Afterwards, a portfolio is created based on the answers entered into the questionnaire. The portfolio developed is based on index-based and low-cost ETFs, which allows robo-advisors to offer complete management of investments at much cheaper rates.

What's more, robo-advisors are a great indulgence for any kind of investor, because they are readily available in spite of the level of capital owned by the investor. The majority of them allow investors to open accounts with as little as a couple hundred dollars or no money at all. In the basic sense, robo-advisors are traditional investment advisors and managers, but aimed at small and growing investors. Some examples of robo-advisors include Betterment, M1 Finance, and Personal Capital.

Online Brokers

These days, the investment climate is rife with full-service, discount brokers, who allow investors to trade entirely online. The key merit of online brokers is that an investor can trade in just about anything that attracts them, including mutual funds, futures, ETFs, bonds, stocks, and options, among several other investment types. Even better, online brokers tend to charge lower commissions per investment, a service particularly intended for the frequent investor. Online brokers work best for self-directed investors with a substantial level of experience in the stock market, who are capable of managing their own portfolios. Online brokers vary in helpfulness, with some of the best offering live assistance and investment tools to aid and improve results for their clientele. Some examples of online brokers are ZacksTrade and E*Trade.

Different Types of Trading

Relative to how much time in a day you can spare to trade and whether you are risk-averse or a risk lover, you can choose from the various trading styles listed below.

Day Trading

Day trading is a safer option for investors who aren't inclined to the intensity of scalp trading and don't intend to hold positions overnight. In day trading, investors may enter and exit any held positions within the same day (unlike position and swing trading) thus decreasing the risk of large swings in the market overnight. At the end of a trading day, investors can close their positions with a loss or gain. Trades of this nature typically hold for varying periods, ranging from minutes to hours. As such, it's imperative to study and analyze the market thoroughly and regularly track positions across a trading day.

Similar to scalp trading, day trading relies on regularly gathering small gains to build profit. Day traders closely observe and study technical and fundamental analysis of the market, using technical indicators like the Relative Strength Index, the Stochastic Oscillator, and the Moving Average Convergence Divergence (MACD) to aid in tracking and identifying market trends and conditions.

Trailing Stop Order

A trailing stop order functions like a stop loss, which commands a security to be sold if its value falls below a certain price. With a trailing stop order, the stop loss price will increase as the value of the security increases. But it will not decrease as the value of the security decreases.

Bracketed Orders Trading

Unlike trailing stop orders, bracketed orders go a step further. Similar to the former, investors can use bracketed orders to set trailing stops as either fixed amounts or percentages below the stock price. It's possible to create an upper limit as well, which when attained will result in sales of stocks. For example, if an investor wishes to trade their Pepsico shares, they can create a bracketed order with an upper limit of $50 per share and a trailing stop level of $5 per share. This bracketed order will act in a similar vein to a trailing stop order, with the $5 trailing stop increasing automatically as the stock price ratchets. The telling difference for bracket order trading is that if and when the price of Pepsico shares reaches $50, the bracketed order will instantly become a market order, which will be executed immediately.

Swing Trading

Contrary to day trading in which investors hold positions for limited time within a day, swing trading investors can hold positions for multiple days, which may sometimes extend to a few weeks. Since positions are available for longer periods, investors need not constantly track market charts and trends to capture short-term movements in the market across a trading day. For this reason, swing trading is a common trading style for investors with other commitments (like a full-time job or holidaying), who like to spare their leisure hours to trade. However, not having to constantly track trends and market movement doesn't mean you get to avoid doing it entirely. It is still important for investors to take some time out of their schedules to analyze the market for knowledgeable trading.

Position Trading

In this type of trading, investors focus on the movement of price in the long-term, seeking the highest potential profits that a major shift in price may offer. As such, position traces tend to last for several weeks, months, or even years. Position traders utilize weekly and monthly charts to assess and predict the market, employing a combination of fundamental analysis and technical indicators to pinpoint potential exit and entry levels into the market. For position traders, any slight pullbacks or fluctuations in price is negligible. This means that they don't track their positions as keenly as other forms of trading, but instead keep an eye out for major trends.

Scalping

Unlike its counterparts, scalping is the shortest type of trading. Scalp traders hold positions for a matter of seconds, with several minutes being the maximum time allowable. Such short-term trades aim to exploit little movements in price within a trading day. The aim of scalping is to make many quick trades with little profit margins. But don't be fooled, profits grow through accumulation from several such trades executed within a trading session. Scalping demands highly liquid markets and tight spreads. For this reason, scalpers only invest in key currency pairs, such as USDJPY, GBPUSD, and EURUSD, due to high trading volume and liquidity. Additionally, scalpers only trade during the busiest periods of a trading day, which is usually within the overlap of trading sessions when volatility and trading volume tends to peak.

Market Order Trading

Market orders are the most common and simple form of stock trading. Market orders represent the willingness of an investor to take a given price presented to them during the execution of an order. For instance, say you want to purchase 120 shares from Facebook. If the stock trades at $150 when a market order is created, it shouldn't be surprising if you are charged a little more or less than the set price, say $151.76 or $150.29.

Overall, stock trading can be fun, but you run the risk of failing when you grow overly excited about an opportunity, especially if it promises more returns. Hence, it's imperative to invest intelligently in things you care about. Not only will your desire to trade and flow with the market, but it will also empower your desire to learn more about the investment and its processes.

Why You Should Only Invest in Things That Interest You

Investing in the stock market can be a daunting and intimidating process, especially given the present climate in which news reports peddle scary stories about millions of seniors being unable to retire or disgruntled TV guests mumbling about dividends. It is little wonder that many people hesitate to take the step and invest in the money market. Otherwise, for the intelligent and confident ones already in the market, the thought of putting hard-earned funds on the line for stocks they don't fully understand or like makes no sense. Truth be told, you could have an upper hand over the professionals at Wall Street if only you invest in your area of interest or expertise.

What makes this method of investing any different from the others? The proof is Warren Buffet, who currently sits on the third ring of Forbes' World's Richest list. Buffet grew his much-acclaimed wealth through the stock market. But he isn't the first or only person to try the market, so what sets him apart? Buffet has a personal rule after "never lose money": never buy into a business you don't understand or are interested in. By understanding a sector of the market or a particular business, you have the edge over others when acquiring its stocks. Sure, your experience of the company or sector may not be financially grounded, but your knowledge and interest could come in handy, especially as there are several things worth investing in on the stock market, such as weather or movies. Bet you didn't know that!

It goes to show that no matter who you are or what your financial status is, there is something on the stock market that might interest you. Also, regardless of what your interest is, your understanding of it can be translated into invaluable information for trading the market. For instance, if you are interested in tech, you will better understand and predict whether or not the fragmentation of Linux makes it a key competitor to Apple's product range. Alternatively, if you worked on offshore oil rigs, you know better than everyone else the companies that are in pole position to experience major growth in another couple of years.

In summary, investing doesn't necessarily have to involve thorough studies of investment firms or banks, although that would be beneficial.

Focusing your choice of stocks on enterprises and industries within your sphere of interest rather than on fiscal projections and obligations increases your chances of making informed decisions. Bear in mind that knowing an industry isn't enough of an excuse to avoid performing more research into the same or rival companies. Even if your insider's secret of a certain stock puts you at the top of the pile, endeavor to hold yourself to performing your due diligence.

Stock Market Terminologies

- Stock exchange: This is a facility in which stocks are listed for trading. It's a meeting ground for enterprises and investors.

- Over-the-counter: Over-the-counter trades are ones involving financial securities not listed on a stock exchange.

- Stock: This is a general term that describes the certificate of percentage of ownership of an enterprise.

- Share market: Share markets are for buying and selling shares. For instance, every stock exchange in the United States is part of the U.S share market, as is any share that can be bought or sold outside of said exchanges.

- Share: Shares are stock certificates of a company. So, for instance, if you own 50 stocks, it means you own shares from several different businesses. Conversely, if you own 50 shares, it means you have a percentage of ownership in a given business.

- Bull market: Bull markets happen when the prices of stocks increase.

- Bear market: Bear markets happen when the market experiences a dip in stock prices.

- Order: Orders are proofs of intention or willingness to sell or acquire shares at certain price points. For instance, you could create an order to purchase 200 shares of Tesla at a maximum price of $20 per share.

- Bid: Bids are the amounts investors are willing to give for a share. Your bid is the amount that you are willing to pay for a share.

- Ask: Asks are the price at which investors are willing to sell shares.

- Bid-ask spread: The bid-ask spread is the fiscal difference between the amount at which shareholders are willing to sell shares versus the amount investors are willing to spend in acquiring those shares. A trade can only be executed when a spread is resolved, meaning the asking and bidding prices have to match.

- Liquidity: Liquidity is the speed or ease with which a stock can be sold. Shares are deemed to be highly liquid if they can be readily sold off or have high trade volumes.

- Trading volume: This is the amount of shares that are traded within a trading day.

- Initial Public Offering (IPOs): IPOs mark the decision of a company to go public. It is the first share listed directly by the company for buying and selling on exchanges. Usually, shares are traded among investors and not the parent company directly.

- Index: This is a standard or reference point portfolio managers and investors alike use in measuring the performance of the market. For instance, Sensex and Nifty are some common benchmarks. If a portfolio gains 10% in returns, it sounds impressive. However, if Nifty returns 12% within a similar timeframe, the previous portfolio performed poorly.

- Portfolio: A portfolio is a collection of the different investments made by an investor.

- Intraday trading: Intraday trading concerns the selling and acquisition of stocks within a trading day, such that every position held is closed before the closure of trading for the day.

- Dividends: Dividends are percentages of profits shared to shareholders by the corporation that owns the shares. Simply put, when companies make profits during a financial year, they owe a certain part of that profit to shareholders. The profit distributed to the shareholders is known as dividends.

It's imperative to carve out a niche for yourself in the stock market and hone your skill sets to better manage your portfolio. Avoid wasting time trying to understand or get good at investments that are beyond your sphere of interest or niche. Ultimately, don't try to force anything or risk sabotaging your chances of profit making before they even manifest. It's normal to get excited when starting out in the stock market. This can send you down a path of chasing leads or forcing deals that aberrate from your general flow. Be patient. The market survived the Dot.com bubble burst and will remain long after you lose all your money. Don't make erratic decisions that would hurt your portfolio. Breathe. Relax. Enjoy the journey of this new experience. The money will come with careful planning and execution.

Chapter 2: Using a Ledger to Track Your Progress

Of the many necessary tools for succeeding in trading, a ledger is possibly the one best friend you will need. It's particular to your style of trading and niche, so it's unlikely that there will be anyone out there with the same trading ledger as you. Additionally, it's a great way to store the numbers of your individual trades. This way, you'll better track the process of your trades, giving you a direct perspective of your performance in the market, which can help you refine your approach over time. As you experience several variations in the mood of the market, a ledger will help you discern what has worked best in different situations.

But owning a ledger isn't the end to managing a successful portfolio. The information collected in your ledger is there for improvements on all fronts. But how can you use it? Quantifying your trades into several aspects can help you see where improvements are most needed. Below, we cover a few tips for improving your trading ledger to allow you more room to control and sharpen your performances.

Maximum Adverse Excursion

Maximum Adverse Excursion (MAE) is the highest distance a stock price rises against your trade entry within the period of trading. With this information, you will be able to track the action of your stop-losses (how much you are willing to lose or gain from an asset before it must automatically be sold) to know if they are loose. When a stop-loss is loose, it means that you have placed the order at a higher level than is necessary for that trading session. Take an average of your MAE across several trades and juxtapose it with the average of your initial stop loss. Divide the value of your average MAE by the average value of your initial stop loss to get a ratio.

R Multiple

This is a pretty common calculation that became mainstream due to the book *Trade Your Way to Financial Freedom* by Van Thorp. In a basic sense, the ratio outlines the amount of loss or profit made with respect to the risk percentage taken on a given trade. Like with MAE, you can also take the mean of your R-multiples to improve performance. In turn, you can also take the average of your loss and profit numbers to see how much your tweaks and improvements have affected your trading.

Comments

Your ledger doesn't have to be restricted to numbers and alone. You can also include comments on the trade you make, why you invested, the management process, and why or how you got out. It also makes sense to comment on your emotions when going into a trade, as well as during and after the trade. Carefully outline the technical and fundamental process that went into the set-up. Your comments need not be elaborate on the entire broad analysis but should just be enough to cover the nuances of the trading environment and technical set-up. Talk about your observations, which fueled trading decisions in managing your investments. What made you tighten your stops or collapse a trade earlier than planned?

It's only logical that our emotions would swing over the course of a trade between the fear of missing out on a trade or the fear of losing money. Instead of ignoring your emotions, identify them and comment on how they might have influenced your bias during decision-making. Such self-awareness is helpful in avoiding impulsive choices caused by emotions; hence, saving you from the risk of poor trading decisions.

Maximum Favorable Excursion

Maximum Favorable Excursion (MFE) is the limit stock prices climb in favor of your entry over the course of a trading session. Unlike MAE that focuses on stop loss, MFE concerns the exit point of a trade—profits. It is a statistic that will help you decipher how much money is left on the table. The data collected into the MFE is best used by traders that utilize discretionary exits from the market rather than waiting for time stops, take profits, or stop-losses to kick in. MFE offers you an evaluation of your reading of the market and your decision to exit trades. So, regardless of whether you favor swing trading or day trading, the information offered by MFE is useful to all for maximizing gains.

What Is a Ledger?

A ledger is a log used to monitor and track trades, as well as their underlying reasons and the eventual outcomes. A ledger can be as simple as a binder purchased from a dollar store in which you note your trade history, or as sophisticated as an in-depth software. Trading journals are especially widespread among investors that focus on complex trades, such as those who trade the foreign exchange market (forex). However, it isn't limited to those types of investors alone, and can also be used by those who trade the options and stock markets. A common erroneous belief about trading ledgers is that they are used for keeping logs alone and tracking profits and loss. That is barely the case. At its core, the goal of using trading journals is to become better at trading and making trading decisions. It's not to keep scores for which to scold or pat yourself on the back with. Ledgers are for learning from both your failures and successes and building better systems and processes for trading. Simply put, it's an analytical system for performing better in the future.

What Goes Into a Ledger?

Although there are lots of good software solutions for ledgering your trades, we'll focus on the orthodox method of using a binder with loose leaves. Binders are better suited for trading ledgers because other materials pertaining to your trades can be easily stored inside.

Some important criteria to note each time you trade include:

- The time and date of entry
- The title (name) of the stock(s) purchased
- The reason for entering each trade
- How you entered the trade (did you utilize any given systems in the process?)
- The emotions experienced before going into a trade and during the period of its life cycle
- The amount of shares acquired and the reason behind the said amount
- Where you created stops
- The position held (is it long or short?)
- The ticker symbol(s) for the stock(s) you bought
- The time and date you left your position(s)
- The reason for closing your trade(s)

- Thoughts on closing your trades (what you would do differently next time and how that could affect the trades you just concluded)

- The percentage loss or gain realized from a session or trading day

How to Make the Most of Your Ledger

Of course, it's a helpful exercise to record the important details of your trades, but the real importance lies in the later part of keeping a ledger: reviewing it. Each week you should take time out to review your trading journal. Sit back in your favorite chair, take off your shoes, and settle down with a good drink. Identify the days of the week that you recorded the most strength. If you constantly worry and sell out your stocks on Tuesdays and Thursdays, it could be an indication that liquidity is a problem. After all, it could be that volume is at its lowest on those days.

But strength isn't the only thing to look out for. You can also figure out the following:

- Which do you experience the most success in: long or short trades?

- What sort of reports or alerts affect you the most and are likely to influence your trading decisions?

- How do you adjust your trading system? Is it in favor of high-priced stocks or lower-priced ones?

- What trade size are you most comfortable with?

- Are there particular periods of a trading day that you experience the most success or loss?

By reviewing your journal regularly, you can find answers to these and several more questions that can help you devise and utilize a better system of trading. It's imperative to apply an analytical perspective when studying your journal. It also helps to be brutally honest about your performances.

Understanding the Difference Between a Ledger and a Budget

Another erroneous belief about ledgers is that they are the same as budgets. Granted, both terms share certain similar concepts, but are distinct in and of themselves. A ledger is a personal logbook for measuring performance, with the sole purpose of identifying trading habits. It can be a digital or physical component for documenting your spending and may be utilized in the creation of budgets. Conversely, a budget is a tool for aligning your spending habits with your values, goals, and priorities. It's a blueprint intended to shape and influence spending decisions, while giving you a general evaluation of your finances. Ledgers and budgets can be used together for providing insight into spending patterns, adjusting and creating financial goals and barriers, and creating future financial plans.

Throughout history, ledgers have taken the form of booklets, which people carried about in their pockets or purse to manually take notes of their expenditures at point-of-sale. In recent years, with innovation fast catching up with the industry, people kept their receipts, which they entered into ledgers (typically Excel documents) on their computers. For others, the summaries or statements of their credit or debit cards serve as rough, automated ledgers. Nowadays, the majority of people make use of websites and software programs that read accounts, collate data, and serve as automated digital ledgers. Such programs tend to act in the capacities of both a ledger and budget, gathering and synthesizing information for decision-making and evaluation.

The Importance of Keeping a Personal Ledger

A ledger can help you identify the chink in your best strategies. Sure, you have undergone and passed the best courses in technical analysis and have put a lot of effort into studying trades and positions. You have given the bulk of your time to preparing for the perfect entry. But no trading strategy is perfect to the core. Not even yours. There are bound to be loopholes. This is especially the case for newbie investors. Experience is a huge part of playing the stock market, so even when you seem technically qualified, a lot could go wrong with your trading strategy. To know and identify these wrongs and loopholes is to study your trades with a strong, keen eye. Here is where your ledger will prove handy. You can easily revise your previous trades, identify what went wrong and find feasible solutions.

Ledgers are also useful for identifying and understanding your strengths and weaknesses. What habits do you exhibit during trading? What are your weakest and strongest points? Having these answers is key to your success. To improve your trades and returns, you must double down on your strengths and make substantial improvements on your areas of weakness. Having a ledger is imperative to this process as it contains all your trading data, outlining the areas you were right in and where you made the wrong calls. By studying your ledger, you can identify patterns and discern your weaknesses and strengths.

You needn't follow the blueprint of other investors exactly. Journals can help you create a unique trading style. There's a reason why blindly following in the footsteps of other traders is a recipe for disaster. Everyone adopts a technique unique to them because the styles, niches, and interests of others may not be yours too. This goes to show why establishing your niche is a core part of getting into the stock market.

What style best fits you? How do you prefer to trade the market? These are some of the answers that you can find in your ledger.

You want to be able to audit your trading sessions. Your journal can help with this. In fact, this is one of the more obvious purposes of using a ledger. When journaling your trading process, it's much easier and seamless to audit your trading decisions. You can study your trade history at any one point and extract relevant information for use in the decision-making process. Auditing is one of the main elements used by stock traders to improve their smarts and techniques.

You will become more accountable with a ledger. During the period of your trading journey, growth and betterment are part of the process, but they won't happen by chance or automatically. To get better results and grow, conscious effort is required on your part. Such a proactive approach is only likely to come when you hold yourself accountable for how your trades turn out. Think of your ledger as a mirror that reflects all the actions you take. There is no escaping the reality of it. If and when you make mistakes, it will be right there in the details.

Your stock trading journal will make you a better trader. In a general sense, the many different benefits of keeping a stock trading ledger culminates into making you a better investor. It improves your discipline and acquaints you with the trading aspect of your personality. In turn, you are wizened to the trading styles that work best for you and learn to play towards and away from your strengths and weaknesses, respectively. Also, you get to chronicle your growth as a trader, getting access to the right data, strategy, and mindset that actively improves your approach and yourself as a trader.

Everything Your Ledger is Going to Help You Track

Within the taxing industry, there is a common maxim: those who keep records win. As an investor, you will likely get involved with several financial securities, such as mutual funds, bonds, options, ETFs, and stocks. When you trade those assets, you will typically aim to maximize your losses and minimize your gains for tax reasons. Counterintuitive, but that's a thing. Your profits or losses can be measured from the tax basis of your investment, making it necessary for you to track the basis of your portfolio. That said, what is the basis? The basis of an investment starts with the ask price paid to acquire the said investment. However, the terms change when investments are acquired through inheritance or gifting. A basis isn't a fixed value, meaning it is subject to change over the period of ownership of the asset and can be influenced by different occurrences. The following sections describe some of the things you can keep track of using your ledger.

Return of Capital

A return of capital is a return made on a percentage of an investment. It's a nontaxable sum, hence it will lower your basis in a security. For instance, if an investor owns 150 shares in IJK Enterprises procured at the rate of $15 per share (totaling $2,250), and the business offers him a $150 nontaxable return capital. The basis of the investor in the stock has reduced by $150. That is, $2,250 - $150 or $14 per share. If, for the duration of ownership, the investor's return of capital grows beyond the investment, the excess becomes taxable. This is because the basis cannot be negative.

Stock Spin-Off

Usually, enterprises tend to spin-off several other businesses. For instance, AT&T broke up some years back into a handful of regional phone companies that later merged with others or spun off into more companies. Every time such events occur in the stock market, the parent company provides investors with accurate documentation of how the prior basis is split across the resulting businesses. It's imperative to keep track of these events as they unfold, as it could help with constructing data as time goes by.

Reinvested Cash Dividends

Investors are typically presented with myriads of opportunities to reinvest dividends rather than cashing out of the system. By giving in to such a plan, investors acquire more shares using taxable returns. Therefore, except for detailed records that are kept of the process, investors may find it difficult to prove how much of their profit was taxable, the percentage of loss deductible, or the amount involved in acquiring additional shares. This is especially necessary for the shares to be sold in the long run.

Broker Fees

While broker charges classify as deductible expenditures, they tend to be accounted for in the majority of transactions involving bonds and stocks. The ask price for a block of stock tends to include the broker fees, while the sales price presented to the IRS (gross returns on sale) is the net value of the cost of sale.

Stock Dividends

Stock dividends can be taxable and nontaxable, and both can be remitted to investors. Taxable stock dividends offer additional stocks to investors, including a basis equal to the said taxable stock dividend. On the flip side, nontaxable stock dividends increase the amount of shares owned by investors, however, the basis doesn't change. Simply put, when investors link their dividends to a given block of stock, the basis of such stocks will be influenced accordingly. Otherwise, the influence will affect the entire holdings of the stock in particular.

Stock Splits

Stock splits can become confusing and overwhelming if you fail to track them as they happen. For instance, say, an investor acquired 150 shares of IJK Incorporated at the rate of $30 per share, paying a total of $4,500. Over time, the business splits the stock 3 for 1; meaning that the investor now has 450 shares to his name. However, the basis in each stock has dwindled to $10 per share.

Mathematically, 450 shares × $10 = $4,500. This is the initial amount he paid to acquire the shares.

Stock splits only occur in situations when the value of stocks per share grows beyond the financial capacity of small-time investors, making it difficult for them to acquire 190 share blocks. It also helps to keep an eye out for reverse splits, whose effects are the exact opposite.

Everything You Need to Know About How to Fill Out a Ledger

When creating a ledger for trading, there are certain data points that are key to the process of journaling your progress. They include:

- Exit price
- Entry price
- Losses
- Profits

But these four data points alone won't suffice, as there are other factors important for your trading performance, such as broad market news, analysis of markets, emotions, macroeconomic reviews, among others. Other vital data for your ledger include but aren't limited to the following:

- Time: The period until expiration of your trading position(s)

- Date: The date you entered or exited a trade

- Stock: The stocks traded at any one point

- Setup: The trading environment that warranted your entry

- Long or Short: The direction of your trades

- Lot size: The size of your trading position(s)

- Stop loss: The price at which you will exit the market if a trade goes bad

- Price out: The price you exited with
- Price in: The price of the stock on entry
- Total cost: The total amount the spread cost
- Loss and Gain: The profit or loss generated by your trades

Best Practices and Knowledge for Evaluating Investment Performance

It's both normal and necessary for investors to pay more attention to the returns generated by their portfolios. Naturally, everyone wants insights into their performance and how much appreciation their investments have undergone over time. Before news became mainstream and accessible around the clock, as well as websites and applications dedicated to minute-by-minute analysis and goings on of the market, investors relied on and were satisfied with positive returns in the long run. However, with the birth and rise of indexes, regular performative comparisons, and benchmark reports, it is more difficult for investors to decipher the best method of evaluating returns in relation to the market as a whole. The problem is that for investors with diversified portfolios, getting a comparative performance evaluation is no simple undertaking.

The first inhibition involves the trouble of choosing the right benchmark that properly reflects the positions in a portfolio. A portfolio composed of several top companies in the United States could implement the S&P 500 as a benchmark, but what happens if the portfolio also contains other securities like international equities and bonds? In such events, several different benchmarks are needed to accurately assess performance. To complicate matters further, a complete performance evaluation must include a risk analysis relative to the benchmark(s) used. Underperforming portfolios, when compared to an index, is allowable for the time being, given that the risk of the portfolio is lower in proportion to the index.

Additionally, a complete and accurate performance evaluation must contain measures of risks and risk-adjusted returns, which are processes that many individual investors are lacking in the necessary tools or experience needed to perform.

So, what do you do as an individual investor if you want an easy benchmark? How do you find out if your portfolio is performing positively?

There are several methods of simplifying the evaluation process while avoiding the risks posed by oversimplification and arriving at wrong conclusions. With reasonable expectations of your portfolio, creating a target return rate in the long term is one of the easiest methods of evaluating performance. Any financial professional can help you create a portfolio that borders around your chosen return rate, given that it isn't unreasonable. This is analysis at its simplest—whether or not the portfolio is performing above or below its target. Bear in mind that your target is an average of your portfolio in the long term. Hence, you must be prorated for the times it under and over performs. Another alternative is to set a pristine benchmark before investing your funds. Pick a benchmark or a collection of benchmarks that reflect the performance of your portfolio the most but remember that your benchmarks will likely change with objectives over time.

Beyond these simpler approaches, individual investors who want deeper insights into their performance are better off conversing with the financial professionals managing their portfolios. Investors will be privy to information, which may include but not be limited to benchmark recommendations and the process of blending them to create an oranges-to-oranges comparison. No discussion about performance evaluation is complete without talking about evaluation frequency. Long-term investors are best served by focusing on performance across several years. A fairly widespread pitfall is for such investors to react poorly to a bad run of form within a month or quarter. In that case, the investor is prone to making wrong alterations in the management of their assets, which may result in poorer performances or outright failure.

In summary, the core of performance evaluation is to target realistic goals, prevent oversimplification, and maintain discipline. If something poses a problem, consider looking into it keenly before deciding on permanent changes.

The following sections describe some other tools for evaluating performance.

Portfolio Standard Deviation

Measuring the standard deviation of your portfolio is one of the most common metrics for evaluating the risk percentage of a portfolio, as well as making relatively precise predictions about performance over time. This calculation considers the returns generated over a specific time frame to decipher the range of possible average returns going forward.

Treynor Ratio

The Treynor ratio, otherwise called the reward-to-volatility ratio, evaluates returns similar to undertaken risks in a comparable method to the Sharpe ratio. However, the telling difference between the methods is that the Treynor ratio considers the volatility of a portfolio instead of its standard deviation.

Sharpe Ratio

The Sharpe ratio is arguably one of the best and most used tools by investors for comparing the amount of returns generated by a portfolio in comparison to its risk percentage. The mathematical approach is quite simple:

Sharpe Ratio = $(Rp - Rf) / \sigma p$
Where:
Rp is the returns generated by the portfolio
Rf is the risk-free rate
σp is the standard deviation of the portfolio

Shortfall Risk

Shortfall risk is a condition in which a portfolio doesn't create returns high enough to meet the target goal. This is a relatively common event, especially in retirement planning, where overt conservativeness and shirking from taking risks or attempting too little risks is more harmful than good to an investor in the end. This is because due to limited risks, the portfolio generated fewer gains than expected.

Beta

Beta is a straightforward risk metric that is typically available to individual stocks and mutual funds by means of a screening tool. The risk metric evaluates the strength of correlation between a benchmark index and an investor's asset(s) or portfolio. A beta of 1 implies that both the benchmark and portfolio are in perfect correlation. However, for every 2% spike or dip in the benchmark, investors can expect to experience similar performances in their portfolios.

Relative Metrics

A relative metric is an evaluation tool that requires comparison to another index or benchmark portfolio like the S&P 500. This provides investors with a gauge for assessing the performance of their portfolio, and gives insight into how well it performed, as well as possible changes that need to be implemented for better performances going forward. Bear in mind that tracking errors may be present in areas where the portfolio and benchmark index start to diverge over time, making comparisons unwise and unhelpful to investors.

Value-at-Risk

Value-at-Risk (VaR) is a metric mostly used by financial institutions for measuring the amount of total risks the business is prone to, as well as the likelihood of those risks occurring. The term is akin to risk-of-loss, which is more applicable to legal or insurance contracts. Risk-of-losses specify the party directly responsible for managing the risk or loss. In terms of portfolio, value-at-risk can be used to evaluate the highest possible loss using a specified probability amount and a defined time frame. For instance, if a portfolio has a (VaR) of 15% on $250,000 across a 12-month period, it means that there is 15% likelihood of the portfolio losing more than $250,000 within a year.

Yield

Yield is a metric expressed in percentage. It is the measure of the income generated by an investment during a given period, usually a year, divided by the cost price of the investment. Every bond generates yields, as do bank accounts (including cash deposits), dividend-paying stocks, and most mutual funds.

Yields on Cash Deposits

If your assets exist as conventional cash deposits, it's relatively easy to determine your yield. The bank or financial institution in charge will provide you with an interest rate on the cash deposit, as well as an annual percentage yield (APY). Most of the time the yield rate is fixed throughout the lifecycle of a cash deposit.

Yields on Bonds

When bonds are acquired at an issue, its yield is similar to its coupon rate or interest rate. The rate is determined by dividing the annual interests generated by the par value, which is typically $1,000. So, if an investor collects $100 worth of interest from a $1,000 bond, the yield is 10%. However, bonds acquired after issuance in the secondary market have a different yield from the initial coupon rate. This change is primarily due to changes in cost price, which differs from the par value. Bond yields fluctuate in accordance to several events, such as the demand of bonds in the market, the credit rating of the issuer, and the interest rate environment.

Yields on Stocks

For stocks, yield is calculated by dividing the year's dividend by the stock's market price. You can find that information online, in the financial pages of your newspaper, and in your brokerage statement. Of course, if a stock doesn't pay a dividend, it has no yield. But if part of your reason for investing is to achieve a combination of growth and income, you may have deliberately chosen stocks that provided a yield at least as good as the market average. However, if you're buying a stock for its dividend yield, one thing to be aware of is the percentage of earnings that the issuing company is paying to its shareholders. Sometimes stocks with the highest yield have been issued by companies that may be trying to keep up a good face despite financial setbacks.

Recording Scenarios

As much as ledgering is gaining traction among new and existing investors, some still do it wrong. It's not uncommon for many investors to only record their entries and exits, the positions held and their respective sizes, and the profits or losses accrued within a trading session or day. By all means, those details are imperative for performance evaluation and the reviewing process now and in the future. However, ledgering goes beyond that, because these details can be found in the trading history of your trading terminal. So technically, it's lazy, pointless record keeping if these details are all you input into your ledger.

Instead of putting conscious effort into irrelevant data, start recording scenarios that are detailed and relevant to your trade. Scenarios don't necessarily imply the entire detail of the trade, although it may sometimes involve this. Just take some time off during a trading day, say, the end of a trading session to record these details. In the same vein, set a time within the week for revising and going through the scenarios. Not only would this help you understand the background of your trading decisions, but the outcomes and performance of your portfolio as well.

There are three main forms of scenarios that are worth tracking and journaling in your ledger.

Opportunities Executed as Trades

Journaling this scenario is technical and could take the form of a template. The time and date of the journal entry can be placed at the top of the page. Next would be the name of the asset as well as the lifecycle of the trading position. Here, you can also include the time frames of the other trades you are monitoring in parentheses. Following in successive orders are the entry price and exit price, as well as the size of the trade in the form of contracts (or whatever variable is used to quantify the volume of your trade). Finally, the starting and ending balances after the trade has been closed comes in next, just ahead of the amount of profit or loss the trade generates.

Beneath these data, you can include snippets of any relevant graphs to your trade. You can stick your graphs to a page, draw it by hand, or label and store it in the pockets of your binder. The graphs might come in handy for annotations that explain the reasoning behind some of your trading decisions, such as placement of stop-loss and point or price of entry. Conversely, you should also include graphs or snippets about the latter parts of the trading session, with annotations to explain your exit point and the market events that ensued afterward. With this knowledge, you will understand if your exit strategy was the best choice at the time.

More commentary about your trading session should follow beneath the graphs and trade snippets. Here, you'll discuss your mindset before and after the trade, money management decisions, the technical analysis involved, and the fundamental analysis as well. In the summary of your fundamental analysis, you will include your reasons (if any) for trading a particular market, including any goings on in the market that you knew could influence the trade. In the technical analysis section, your entry should revolve around your reasoning for entering a trade based on chart analysis and the outcome; did it fit your system or not? The third column should contain your money management decisions, including the amount at risk while trading and the potential profit.

Finally, describe your mindset and emotions during the trade. Were you emotionally neutral or biased when entering, exiting, or during the lifecycle of positions held? At the bottom right corner of the page, you can add your final thoughts on the scenarios. Did you think you did well or could've done better? What would you like to remind yourself when going into another trade?

Opportunities Not Executed as Trades

For this scenario, journaling will be similar to the opportunities executed as trades. Except in this case, the trade is gone, and your journaling would be from a point of narration. Where would you have entered or exited the market? While detailed journaling is necessary here, you also want to show that it's not a real trade that was executed. This will help prevent confusion or fiscal imbalances that may arise in the future. When painting the scenario of such trades, it helps to include an extra section at the end explaining why you didn't execute the trade, if it was an opportunity missed, and why you should have taken it. Also, details like what you might do differently in the occurrence of such trades in the future is important.

Interesting Situations That Occur on the Market

In this scenario, it's necessary to have pictorial references of the different things that took place in the market over the duration of your trades. You want to target moments such as: how the market reacted to news releases, the time alterations occurred in market activities, the different types of markets experienced during trading sessions, the various candle setups involved, and variations in significant levels. The aim is to create a database of the different scenarios that caught your interest that you feel are worth looking into for better knowledge of the market. In your gathering of pictorial references (screenshots, printed graphs, etc.), ensure to include annotations. This will prevent confusion and allow for better journaling in your ledger.

Below each pictorial reference, you can include details like fundamental analysis, technical analysis points, the reasons why the said scenario interests you, how you'd react to it in the future, if you would enter it as a trade, and how you would track such situations going forward. Aim to curate qualitative data for your references to provide you with insights in the future. This is especially necessary when you attempt to optimize your approach with those scenarios as filters to prevent certain effects or influence your trades in a particular way.

Keeping records of your investment dealings is a habit that will greatly pay off as you go. The ability to reference your previous approaches and their respective outcomes will offer you lots of insights, giving you an edge over your contemporaries. Additionally, it will improve your learning rate, especially as a beginner, as you will have a platform for reviewing and understanding your choices and why things turned out the way they did.

Chapter 3: Establishing the Best Investment and Trading Strategies for You

The stock market is a huge vehicle of large and diverse moving parts, which are constantly in random motion. This can make it confusing to the average investor, especially one who aims to grasp the entirety of it. To succeed, it's necessary to have a narrower view of this larger-than-life vehicle and focus on specific areas of it. This is where niches and areas of interests come into the picture. By focusing on these areas, you will establish expertise and can strive to be the best within the little bubble you're comfortable in. Simply put, don't try to be a jack of all trades.

Different Types of Investing Strategies

In view of the types of stocks discussed in Chapter One, let's consider some investing strategies for earning from those stocks.

Growth Investing

Growth investing focuses on investments that have strong upside potentials in terms of returns of stocks in the future. Simply put, growth investors are ones who are on the lookout for the next big thing on the market. However, this doesn't mean that growth investing is a reckless process of predictive trading. On the contrary, it involves keen evaluation of the present health of a stock, as well as its growth potential in the long term. For this approach to work, growth investors study the prospects of the industry that a stock thrives in. For instance, if you want to explore the stocks of Tesla, you would typically do your homework on the future of electric vehicles. Alternatively, if you lean toward artificial intelligence, you may ponder the likelihood of it becoming a mainstay in day-to-day life before investing in the stocks of its industry.

Proof of robust and widespread use and demand for the products or services of a business is necessary if the enterprise is to grow. Investors answer their questions by evaluating the history of a company. In simpler terms, a growth stock ought to grow. The business listing the stocks must show consistency with strong, stable revenue and earnings, implying their ability to deliver on expectations of growth. However, straightforward as it might seem, growth investing isn't without its drawbacks. One key downside to investing in growth stocks is the absence of dividends. Companies in growth mode require huge capital to fuel and sustain development and expansion. During this process, not much is left (if any) to be distributed to shareholders as dividends. Besides, the faster the return rate and growth, the higher the valuations, which may prove to be a risky indulgence for many investors.

Value Investing

Value investing is a form of bargain shopping in which investors comb the market for stocks believed to be undervalued. They seek out stocks priced at rates they believe don't entirely capture the intrinsic or potential value of the asset. On one hand, value investing is predicated on the logic that there is a measure of irrationality in the general market. In theory, this irrationality is an opportunity to acquire stocks at discounted prices and earn profits. Value investing doesn't necessarily involve investors sifting through volumes of data for the perfect deals. There are tons of value mutual funds, which present investors with the chance to own lots of stocks deemed to be undervalued. For instance, the Russell 1000 Value Index is a common benchmark used by value investors. What's more, several mutual funds are tailored to mimic it.

As always, investors can alter their trading strategies at any point, but such decisions can prove costly, especially in value investing. Regardless, lots of investors have given this strategy the boot following a run of poor performances over the years. Jason Zweig, a Wall Street Journal reporter, explained in 2013 that over the turn of the last decade, value funds that specialized in large stocks generated about 6.7% in returns per year on average. However, the average investors in such funds only earned 5.5% at the end of the year. The underlying reason for this disparity in earnings traces back to the fact that most investors pulled out their investments over time. It goes to show that the only way to get the most out of value investing is go play for long-term goals.

Dollar-Cost Averaging (DCA)

Dollar-cost averaging is the process of regularly investing in the market as time goes by, with no mutual exclusivity to any of the other strategies discussed in this section. Simply put, dollar-cost averaging is a strategy concerned with executing any strategy chosen by the investor. With DCA, an investor could decide to make a $300 deposit to an investment account monthly. Such a disciplined approach to investing can pay well, especially if the investor uses automated features to manage their portfolio. This is because committing to a plan is much easier when little to no oversight is required in the process. The upside of using the DCA approach is that it steers clear of ill-fated and hurtful strategies about market timing. Even the most experienced investors aren't above the temptation of buying stocks when prices decrease only to find out, and painfully too, that the prices dip even further over time.

When investments occur in regular increments, investors can capture prices at different levels, from low to high. In essence, the periodic investment involved in DCA is helpful in decreasing the average purchase costs per share. To implement the DCA strategy, three key parameters must be decided:

1. Capital: How much will be invested?
2. Frequency: How regularly will purchases be made?
3. Timeframe: How will investments be made with respect to time?

Dollar-cost averaging is considered a healthy investment strategy for many investors because it helps build commitment to saving while decreasing the influence of volatility and risk potential. On the flip side, DCA isn't a good choice for people who intend to invest lumps of capital at once.

Momentum Investing

Momentum investing involves riding the waves of the market. In this strategy, investors believe that market losers will continue to lose and vice versa. These investors aim to acquire stocks that are on the uptrend due to the belief that losers will continue dipping. As such, they could decide to short sell such securities. But short selling is not a guaranteed route with no risks. Momentum investors can be pictured as technical analysts. Meaning, they strictly adhere to a data-driven process of trading and study stock prices for patterns that influence their trading choices. Essentially, momentum investors trade without regard for the efficient-market hypothesis (EMH). This hypothesis posits that the prices of assets are a complete reflection of the available information known by the public. This postulation is hard to stomach for any momentum investor given that their strategy aims to capitalize on equities that are over or undervalued.

Types of Stock Investment Opportunities and Their Respective Benefits

When you think of stock trading, you probably imagine investors purchasing shares in rising companies and making profits when such companies increase in value. But there are more ways to invest in the stock market than that. You can, in fact, look at the stock market as a part of your retirement plan.

Consider the various stock trading opportunities below.

Individual Stocks

When investing in individual stocks, you are directly acquiring a percentage of ownership of a business. That is, if you invest in 300 shares of a publicly traded enterprise, you own a certain percentage of the business. When companies go public, their aim is to sell shares to investors to generate capital for starting, growing, or expanding the business. Once the first shares have been acquired, they can then be traded on exchanges or electronically between sellers and buyers under the facilitation of stockbrokers. You earn from this ownership through dividends, which are premiums issued by the company to its shareholders. Another method of earning is via appreciation of stock prices.

Pros

With individual stocks, it's easier to understand your portfolio, because you're responsible for choosing your stocks. Hence, you have total control over what you invest in and the timing of the investment. It's much easier to manage taxation on individual stocks because you are only charged at the point of sale. Thus, you can manage the timing to reduce losses or collect gains. Investing in individual stocks means lower fees. You wouldn't have to make annual remittances as management charges for investing your portfolio. Rather, you are only charged a fee when acquiring the stock and at point of sale. For the remainder of the time, there are no added fees. Also, the longer the stock remains in your ownership, the less it costs you.

Cons

Diversifying your portfolio is harder with individual stocks when money is limited. So, the moment you begin investing, you've indirectly bought into the risk posed by lack of diversity.

Investing in individual stocks involves keeping a leash on your emotions. It's much easier to acquire a hot-tip stock or sell a loser because trading can be done in a matter of minutes. This can significantly spike trading fees and lock in losses, which could have been avoided by holding your position for longer.

Individual stocks require more time and effort to monitor your assets. You have to ensure that the businesses you invested in aren't experiencing problems that could make your stocks dip or become worthless. For this reason, it's imperative that you constantly keep a finger on the buzz of economic and industrial trends. In essence, the sole responsibility of managing your portfolio is in your hands, so you have to devote your time and resources to ensure you aren't holding the wrong position.

To adequately diversify your portfolio, you need between 20 and 100 stocks. Based on portfolio theory you are taking on more risks by diversifying, so you may just be better off owning a handful.

Mutual Funds

Mutual funds are financial vehicles composed of money pooled together by several investors to acquire securities such as money market instruments, bonds, and stocks. Mutual funds are managed by professional money managers whose jobs revolve around allocating the assets procured by the funds to generate income or capital gains for investors. The portfolios of mutual funds are maintained and tailored to match the investment goals recorded in its prospectus.

Mutual funds allow individual or small-time investors to access portfolios of bonds, equities, and other securities that are professionally overseen. As a result, every shareholder is a participant in the losses or gains the fund generates. Since mutual funds are invested in a variety of securities, performances are evaluated and tracked as any alteration in the total market cap of the asset. This can be determined by finding the aggregate of the performances of the constituent investments.

Pros

Mutual funds are traded on some of the biggest stock exchanges. This makes buying and selling them quite easy. As such, if you are concerned about being able to pull your money out of an investment, mutual funds are as liquid as they come.

Diversification is perhaps the biggest upside of mutual funds, as the diversification of assets and investments helps to reduce the risk quotient of a portfolio. Experts suggest diversification as a means of improving the returns of a portfolio.

Mutual funds are under the coverage of industry regulations, which ensure that fairness and accountability is extended to every investor involved. With mutual funds, investors can study and pick from a variety of managers with different management goals and approaches. For example, a fund manager's style could revolve around income, growth investing, emerging markets, developed markets, macroeconomic investing, or value investing.

Alternatively, a different manager could also oversee a portfolio that implements many different strategies. Such variety enables investors to garner exposure beyond bonds and stocks to other securities, such as foreign assets, real estate through special mutual funds, and commodities.

Cons

Studying and comparing stocks can be an arduous task. Contrary to stocks, mutual funds don't allow investors to compare and contrast sales growth, earnings per share (EOS), or the price to earnings (P/E) ratio, among other vital data.

While mutual funds allow investors to liquidate their shares at any point, the process is anything but swift. For starters, unlike regular stocks which are traded throughout a trading day, most mutual funds can only be redeemed at the end of a trading day.

Similar to other investments without guaranteed rates of returns, the likelihood of depreciation of a mutual fund is high. Equity mutual funds are no strangers to fluctuations in price, including the constituent stocks of the fund. Investments in mutual funds are not backed up by the Federal Deposit Insurance Corporation (FDIC) therefore the guarantee of performance of any fund isn't there.

Since professional management is necessary for mutual funds, the cost of running is quite high. These charges lower the overall returns generated by the fund and are charged to every investor despite how the fund performed on the market.

When fund managers sell their securities, it triggers capital gains taxes. Investors who are bothered about the effect of taxation need to take cognizance of such charges before investing in mutual funds. However, taxation can be mitigated by holding non-tax sensitive mutual funds in tax-deferred accounts such as IRAs or 401(k)s. An alternative technique is to invest in tax-sensitive mutual funds.

Exchange Traded Funds (ETFs)

ETFs are known as exchange traded funds because they can be bought and sold on exchanges like regular stocks. The share prices of ETFs tend to alternate over the course of a trading day as shares are traded on the market. This is a sharp contrast to mutual funds, which can only be traded once each trading day after the market is shut down. In addition, ETFs are a more liquid and cost-effective alternative to mutual funds. But like mutual funds, ETFs can hold several different underlying assets at once, unlike stocks that hold only one. For this reason, ETFs are a popular choice for investors looking to diversify their portfolios.

Pros

It's not unlikely for investors to seek portfolio exposure in specific countries, industries, styles, or sectors without expertise in those areas. Given the vast range of industry, sector, country, and style categories available in ETFs, their shares could easily provide investors with quick exposure into a given market segment of interest.

The running costs for ETFs are common to all kinds of managed funds despite the variety of structure. These costs could include, but aren't limited to, distribution, administrative expenses, portfolio management fees, marketing expenses, and custody costs. Historically, operating costs have played a key role in predicting returns. For example, the lower the running costs of investing in an ETF, the higher the predicted returns of the fund.

ETFs can be acquired and sold during a trading day when the market is open. ETF share prices remain continuous across normal exchange periods. However, share prices may fluctuate throughout a trading day due to alternations in the intraday values of underlying assets that comprise the fund. Hence, investors can find out the price paid to purchase ETF shares within moments, as well as how much was generated from selling shares.

In comparison to mutual funds, ETFs have two main tax advantages. Owing to difference in structure, mutual funds tend to trigger higher capital gains taxes than exchange traded funds. Additionally, the capital gains taxed on ETFs is only triggered when investors sell off the fund, whereas capital gains taxes are enforced on investors throughout the lifecycle of a mutual fund.

Cons

ETFs are characteristically illiquid, and this could pose a real problem if you are more interested in short-term trading. ETFs can be single-industry focused, which largely limits diversification and increases risks. Finally, ETFs can command relatively higher fees if they are actively managed.

Best Stocks to Invest in and Why

Value Stocks vs Growth Stocks

Value stocks do not necessarily sell for cheap, although one of the go-to places for such stocks is the list of securities that have hit 52-week lows. Value investors think of these stocks as bargain trades. The prices of value stocks tend to be low due to undervaluation by the market for several reasons. Investors go into these trades with the intent of acquiring lots of stocks before the prices are corrected in the market. Undervaluation occurs when the price-to-earnings ratio of a stock is in the bottom 10% of stock listings. Securities that fall into this class are deemed value stocks because they are likely to experience a price surge in the future.

Some key features to look out for in value stocks include:

- The current ratio
- The price-to-earnings growth (PEG) ratio
- The tangible book value vs the share price
- The debt-to-equity ratio
- The price-to-earnings (P/E) ratio

On the flip side, growth stocks are securities that can potentially outperform a particular subsegment of the market or the general market as a whole over a period. They have some characteristics of their own, including:

- Projected stock prices
- Earnings per share
- Strong growth
- Earnings before taxes
- Return on equity

For a security to be considered a growth stock, it must have a historical background and future projection of strong growth rate. In the last half of this decade, investors have been more likely to look for growth rates of five to seven percent for larger businesses, and ten percent or more for smaller businesses.

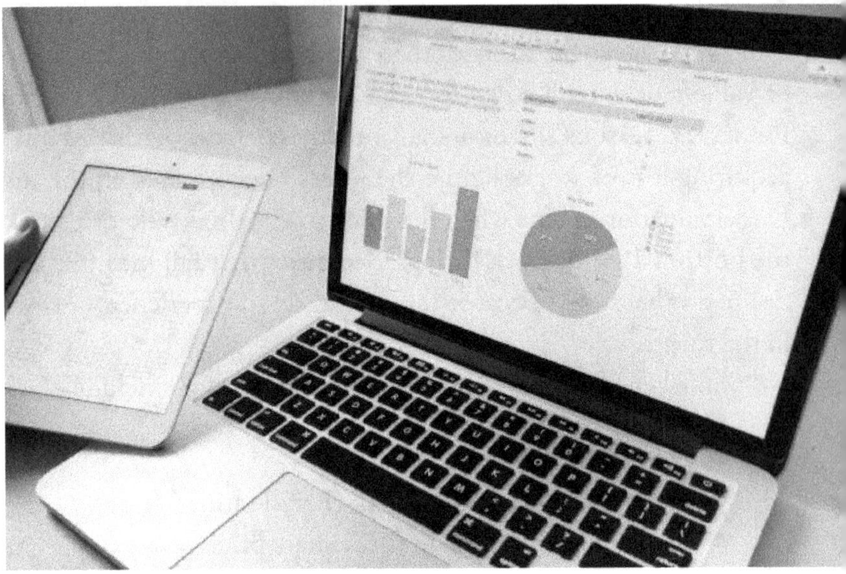

Which Is Better?

In comparison, the historical performances of both growth and value stocks can be evaluated based on the amount of volatility, the time horizon involved, and the risk potential undertaken to achieve those performances.

In theory, value stocks can be considered low risk, although this feature comes at the risk of low volatility as the securities are discovered among bigger and more established businesses. Besides, even when value stocks fail to achieve the target prices predicted by investors or analysts, they still pay dividends and may yet offer capital growth.

Meanwhile, growth stocks will withhold paying dividends to investors, instead choosing to reinvest the retained earnings into the expansion of the business. The likelihood of loss for investors in growth investing is far greater, especially if the company fails to keep up with the growth projections of its shareholders.

High-Yield Stocks

A high-yield stock is a type of security with a higher dividend yield than the yield of a benchmark average. High-yield stocks are classified based on relative criteria. As such, there is no defined template or yardstick for determining if a dividend yield qualifies as low or high. High dividend yields are indicative of undervaluation of a stock, since the dividend generated by the stock exceeds the ask price of the security. Value and income investors are particularly keen on high-dividend yields. It's no surprise, because high-yield stocks almost always outperform their low-yield counterparts in bear markets. Also, many investors consider stocks that pay dividends as less riskier investments.

Avenues of Portfolio Management and Their Respective Benefits

Online Brokers

Online brokers are platforms that facilitate the buying and selling of financial securities over electronic frameworks. Transactions are typically carried out using the proprietary trading platforms of the brokers, as opposed to the traditional method of executing orders through phone calls.

Online brokers exist to exclude favoritism and personal bias from trading. Some have even been found guilty of promoting partnered mutual funds with no regard for investor welfare. Moreover, online trading is more convenient, as trading decisions such as making changes, checking quotes, and placing orders can be done from anywhere. Also, online brokers facilitate faster execution of trades; thus, helping to seize market volatility in a better, timelier way. Perhaps the most significant benefit is that online trading is cheaper and more cost-effective than traditional trading.

Investment Management Professionals (Traditional Advisors)

The past decade has seen a surge in the adoption of technology for more and more activities, including trading, which has called into question the usefulness of traditional advisors. However, the unique structure of the stock market has shown that trust and human relationships may outweigh the benefits of certain technological disruptions. Investing is a matter of personal psychological security because it involves money. Retitling accounts, coordinating income streams, managing estate documents and life insurance policies, and investment reallocations are difficult undertakings for anyone. During such events, traditional advisors could help provide clarity and comfort.

Additionally, financial advisors bring certain values to their relationship with a client, including offering advice instead of solely focusing on portfolio management and asset allocation. Money affects people's lives in more ways than investments. Of course, robo-advisors may charge less and offer relatively faster services, but their value in comparison isn't apples-to-apples with traditional advisors. The services of financial advisors span across everything from purchasing a house to ensuring designated beneficiaries are regularly updated on legacy wishes. Also, financial advisors tend to focus on the long-term goals of their clientele and how best to meet those goals. Their plans could include cash flow, taxes, Medicare, social security, and debt management.

Robo-Advisors

Robo-advisors are digital frameworks that automate financial planning services based on algorithms with little or no human supervision. Their services range from security features, accounting, to goal planning and portfolio management. However, there are a few things to keep in mind about robo-advisors. Robo-advisors provide financial services but not expert planning, which can be key to success. Robo-advisors may not safeguard investors from the risks of forgetfulness or trading decisions like buying high, selling low, or panicking and making impulsive decisions. Simply put, they offer services, not guidance. Robo-advisors are low-cost solutions and work better for new investors, as decreased running costs leave more money to be invested.

Understanding Basic Trading Strategies

Trading strategies are designed to improve the chances of an investor's success and help them manage the risks involved in stock investment. The strategies listed below are some of the most common and effective.

Swing Trading

Swing trading focuses on harnessing the movements of the market for profits, with the aim of buying or selling securities that are projected to rise or fall in value.

Pros

- Swing trading only works as a hobby and is best suited to people with little trading time.
- There are lots of trading opportunities in swing trade, as investors can gain from both sides of the market, going long or short on several securities.

Cons

- Holding overnight positions could incur trading risks, which can be avoided by using stop-losses.
- Swing trading requires keen research to understand and evaluate the market properly. This can be quite tasking for the investors with little time for trading.

Day Trading

Day trading works best for traders who like to actively trade during the day, taking advantage of any fluctuations in price throughout the period the market opens and closes.

Pros

- Day trading comes with lots of opportunities. Investors can harness local and international markets, opening and closing several positions during daytime.

- There is no overnight risk because no trades are left running overnight.

- Daytime risk is limited because day trading is a short-term trading strategy that lasts anywhere between one to four hours.

Cons

- Discipline is necessary for success in day trading. Due to the market risks, investors need predetermined strategies, complete with edit and entry levels.

- Day traders can experience flat trades, which is a phenomenon in which positions are unchanged throughout a trading day. Flat trades are pretty rife and can be overwhelming over time.

Scalp Trading

The aim of scalping is to make little profits from several trades. For this strategy to work, discipline is imperative as any delay in exit may incur huge losses that could trump previous gains.

Pros

- Overnight risks are low because scalping doesn't involve holding positions overnight, with most trades lasting several minutes at most.

- The opportunities for trading are enormous. Unlike other strategies, scalpers can open lots of positions using less defined criteria.

Cons

- Scalping can be a tense endeavor as investors continuously track any minute movement in price in order to make profits. New traders are better off avoiding it.

- Scalping has limited applicability in the market and only works in specific areas, like indices, U.S equities, some bonds, and cryptocurrencies.

- Scalping is best used as a hobby, not as a major trading strategy.

Position Trading

Position trading involves identifying the successive lower highs and higher highs of an asset to determine its trend in the market. Position traders ride the trend wave with the aim of gaining from dips and spikes in the market.

Pros

- Position trading is useful as a hobby and best suits investors with limited time after creating a trend identification system.

- There are lots of trading opportunities. A strong trend could provide investors with multiple opportunities to enter and exit the market, while earning from the movement of the market in either direction.

Cons

- Position trades can be open for several days at a time, so the likelihood of overnight risks is high.

By studying and understanding this chapter, you should already have a method of trading in mind, including choosing an avenue of managing your assets and how to go about it.

What type of stocks interest you the most? How would you prefer to manage your time and resources? Would you like to collaborate with others or go solo? It's important to establish a system that is the right fit for you, and not to get too caught up in what you "should" or "shouldn't" be doing.

Chapter 4: Expanding Your Investment Knowledge and Network

You might hear people talking about making high value connections and growing your network of business leaders, investors, and colleagues. This is because networking is probably the single most important business strategy. You will need to apply it when you get started and continue to network as a way to maintain steady growth or even recover from a fall.

The fact that you are introverted or just have poor social skills matters very little in this instance. Networking is an irrefutable law in business. It is, in fact, an investment within an investment. You might have financially invested in your business or in stocks. But you will also have to invest in building valuable relationships as one of the pillars of your financial investments.

The Importance of Building and Expanding Your Network

For many reasons, networking is one of the most important aspects of becoming a successful investor. First of all, trust is the gateway to lucrative business opportunities. There is so much that you will never know without networking with successful and experienced investors. How to diversify your portfolio, what investments to use as a hedge against inflation and other unforeseen circumstances, and when to invest in certain asset classes are just a few of the protected pieces of information that are freely shared within a network.

Take the real estate market for instance. There is a wealth of dynamic and fresh knowledge to be gained through dialogues with other real estate investors. You could learn about which markets are hot, the ones that will only depreciate, and high-net-worth individuals who are looking to sell some properties. You are unlikely to get this quality of investment education and opportunities anywhere else. As such, it isn't enough to meet people and start a conversation. You must be committed to building trustworthy and long-lasting relationships.

For each contact you add to your network, you are likely to know other people of the same caliber. When you get out and begin to form relationships with individuals who can positively contribute to your goals, you will find people with wide networks. Although it will take some time to get people to share their contacts with you, it will eventually get to this level. This is a huge benefit of networking. It means that you will be more likely to get help, since you will have a broad list of contacts to call on.

Oftentimes, we trust the expertise of other people not based on what they know or have personally achieved, but on the people we see them with. Simply by associating with individuals that we respect or are a fan of, we can decide that certain people must be worth our time and money. But 'association' in this context refers to more than having high-caliber individuals in your photo and being in the same party with them. If you have built a relationship with such people, they could endorse and validate you as a business owner or investor. This endorsement could both encourage other high-caliber individuals to invite you into their circle and, as an investor, attract businesses to you.

Whether you want to believe it or not, there are certain behaviors and habits that increase an individual's chances of success. Usually, the best way to learn these behaviors is by emulating successful people. Even reading books on how you should and shouldn't act are rarely ever as effective as closely observing experienced and wealthy investors and business people. You might even find that you don't necessarily have to deliberately copy the actions of successful people to adopt their habits. You need only frequently interact with them.

The more time you spend with successful investors, the more confident you will become about your financial decisions. This is a natural progression of maintaining the right network. This is because you will not only receive good advice, you will also be able to do things that are impossible if you approach investing and business on your own. You'll be able to compare the suggestions of several investors and figure out what would truly work. Probably the most beneficial aspect of this approach is that you can watch how the advice from different members of your network plays out when they apply it. This sharpens your own instincts and makes you confident in the investment strategies that you choose.

Even though there is a lot that you could gain from your network, it also offers you the opportunity for altruistic investment in other people. This could be by way of mentoring less experienced investors or financially supporting members of your network. Satisfaction and happiness do not only come by receiving help. You can enjoy these same feelings when you give back. In fact, it is nearly impossible to enjoy longevity as an investor or business person by perpetually withholding help. Should you become known for this, you could be excluded from your network—however slowly this happens.

How to Build Your Network

With networking, especially when you are trying to connect with serious investors, you shouldn't just throw your net wide and hope it catches as many fish as possible. Don't attend numerous networking events and give your contacts to every investor you see. You should, instead, be precise about the people you interact with. They should be seasoned investors who do not only possess a wealth of knowledge but would be willing to share it with you.

If you don't know about networking events and other occasions where you could make connections, then you can start from social media. Create a profile that reflects your qualifications, values, and business. Then, reach out to the kind of people who you believe can positively impact your business. LinkedIn is a great place for networking, since you can easily find people who are in the same field of business as you.

When you eventually identify the kind of investors that you would like to connect with, make sure that the time you spend interacting with them is mutually beneficial. This is why it is important that you educate yourself and have some level of experience in your chosen field before networking. You don't want to create a situation where the other person feels cheated.

Connecting with a friend of a friend is usually more successful than trying to network with total strangers. As such, you should ask those you are already close to for the contacts of individuals who would be helpful to your venture. Remember that when you do meet these contacts, you will also be representing the person who referred you, so you should try to make a good impression.

In fact, before you seek advice of any kind from the person you are networking with, you can improve your chances of building a long-term relationship by giving something first. Be the first to share information and offer help. Of course, this would have to be solicited or you might seem arrogant and obnoxious.

This works because people often go to networking events and other similar occasions either expecting to be asked for help or to seek help themselves. However, when you start out by being supportive it makes the other person more responsive to connecting with you.

What type of relationship are you hoping to build with your contacts? You must decide on an answer to this question before you go networking. Are you looking for a mentor, business partner, or client? When your purpose for networking is clearly defined, it will enable you to seek out the right people and interact with them in a way that furthers your goal.

Never resort to speaking negatively about your competitors or those of the individual you are trying to connect with. Don't start off by criticizing strategies or the actions of popular investors. You may not know which way your conversation partner leans regarding certain opinions. But more importantly, you don't want them to think that you could potentially bad-mouth them to other people.

Staying in contact with people, regardless of distance, is just as important as initially approaching them. This is one aspect of networking at which many people fail. It doesn't end at the exchange of contact details. It can seem somewhat underhanded when you only reach out to contacts in your time of need. You should occasionally check in on the people in your network, even if it is just to ask how they are doing.

In fact, you should consider networking even when you don't presently need the help. This way, you can be more focused on building long-term relationships, instead of seeing people as a means to an end.

Bring a wingperson to networking events. This can be especially helpful if you are shy or introverted. You will be more likely to approach strangers and start a conversation when your friend is close by. You will also feel relaxed and able to present the best version of yourself. It is even better if your wingperson is at the event for the same purpose as you. This way they won't feel left out when you try to connect with other people, and you won't waste time chatting with your friend.

Even though you are hoping to expand your network to include highly experienced and financially successful individuals, you should never lose your self-respect and sense of self-worth to be likeable or accepted. You should, of course, be polite, but you also want to be knowledgeable about the business that you are involved in and carry yourself with dignity. You want to build relationships that are founded on mutual respect.

While it is advised that you leave your comfort zone and expand your network by meeting up with successful people, you can also attract them to you by expressing informed and in-depth opinions about your field of investment. If you make investments in the technology sector or have a business in this industry, you should find a way to be constantly updated on the latest tech developments. Share your views and create a community around this subject.

The Importance of Expanding Your Investment Knowledge

The common belief is that attending lectures or paying for online courses are not only time consuming, but require a lot of money. First, not all courses are expensive. Some are either quite affordable or even free. However, even those ones that cost a bit of money still have their merits. There are truly costly mistakes or just time-wasting methods that you would be able to avoid if you spent money to acquire knowledge.

Expanding your network improves your ability to think. We all are limited by the amount of information we have on any subject. If all you have to go on is the linear style of thinking that you were taught in school, you could find out-of-the-box, dynamic reasoning quite difficult or impossible. With things like investments and growing a business, you need to be able to mentally adapt to the constantly changing circumstances.

You can also improve your creativity through expanding your network. When one is described as creative, it simply means that they are able to come up with new solutions and create new strategies from the challenges they are given. To be a creative investor, you need to possess more than a foundational knowledge about the possible challenges that you could be faced with. You need to know what has been tried, and why new solutions are required. Otherwise, you could be excited about what would eventually be revealed as a dud of an idea, or just arrive at the same old solutions as other investors before you.

Finally, expanding your network helps you retain investment knowledge. One of the best ways to make the short-term memory of what you learned into a long-term memory is by teaching. However, people might be unwilling to learn from you if they feel like you don't really know much. Expand your knowledge and by mentoring others, you can stay sharp.

The Basics of Stock Trading

In today's stock trading world that is filled with trading apps, minute by minute price charts, and several individuals promising market signals for a fee, it is tempting to view stock trading as a short-term bet.

However, this perspective greatly increases your chances of losing every bit of your investment. While there are sometimes short-term term gains to be made, one must never rely on this alone. This is an especially important lesson for newbies in the world of stock trading.

Betting on a current trend is much safer than predicting a turn. This is because regardless of how stable or volatile your preferred industry is (whether you are trading Bitcoins or gold), stocks are characteristically irrational. The amount of information you have, and the projections made by respected investors are often futile in determining the rise and fall of stocks. Trends are usually more likely to continue than change. So, in deciding on the best time to place a trade, you should try to identify a trend, ride its coattails, and get out of that position after you've made some profits.

Be careful about your source of information. If you wanted a diagnosis for a symptom you've been experiencing, you wouldn't go to an athlete or visit a fashion website. And even if these sources offer their prognoses, you wouldn't trust them—hopefully. This is because it takes someone in the medical field years of painstaking study and dedication to become qualified. Although the stock market might not be as delicate as medicine, you are still expected to only seek and follow the counsel of time-tested and successful traders. The fact that a particular investor is your friend isn't enough reason to follow their advice.

In many cases, investors fail because they hope that a particular loss would, given enough time, yield profits. But, as stated in the point above, existing trends are likely to continue for longer than you can afford. To be a successful investor, you must know when to give up on a particular trade. Even new investors make profits a lot of the time. However, if you wait until you have lost 25% of your investment, a 33% gain will only help you break even. You must think about the likelihood that your position will improve enough for you to gain 33% and above. Enjoy your wins, don't get carried away, and cut your losses early.

There are quite a number of tools available to modern stock traders that it can be tempting to want to use as many of them as you can at once. The problem is that many of these tools report different information, such that trying to figure out your next move can be stressful. It could, in fact, stall and cost you opportunities. The solution is to keep things as simple as you can. Don't analyze the market with relative strength index, moving averages, moving average convergence divergence, and Bollinger bands all at the same time. All you really need to do is keep your eyes on the trends and use, at most, two indicators.

You cannot win all the time. This is something you must keep in mind, especially if you are trading for the first time. There are numerous characters both offline and online who would have you believe that by paying for their courses or getting trading signals from them you can make profits every single time. Even the most experienced and successful investors do not enjoy this kind of luck. This is because each trade is affected by a number of factors that are not just extremely difficult to predict with any accuracy, but impossible to control. The emotions and desires of every investor involved is one factor. Throw in government policies, natural disasters, the abundance of certain materials and products, demand and supply, and socioeconomic changes, and you can see why price charts are always messy. Prepare to lose a few times (or more).

Many investors consider stock valuation when making the decision to buy or sell. Should a stock be undervalued or have its fair value higher than its trading value, it would be wise to buy this stock—ideally, of course. Conversely, if the fair value of a stock is lower than its trading value, then it is overvalued and selling it is usually the right call. However, it's human beings like yourself who will determine whether a particular stock will continue trading at its overvalued price or fall. As such, you can have stocks that defy every prediction and remain overvalued for a long time.

Sure things are creatures of myth in the stock trading world. They are nonexistent, as they have always been. Many of the companies and stock options that were considered sure things, like ESPN, Alibaba, oil, and gold have all been subjected to the same irrational and unpredictable price movements that are characteristic of the stock market. This is another reason to diversify your investment. Typically, long-term investments in blue chip companies, for instance, will lead to profits. But this is still a risky bet. Things could take a bad turn at the time you need the money.

After spending any amount of time trading stocks, you will learn that many of your preconceived notions are just myths. One common myth is that an investor can be highly intuitive when it comes to detecting successful companies. However, this intuition often relies on the branding and marketing of the company. You can't just take a brand's word that they are performing well. Due diligence is required to uncover the true financial performance of any company and the risks involved when you invest with them. You can start your search from the regulatory filings that public companies are required to submit to the SEC either quarterly or annually. These filings also contain records of managerial changes and acquisitions.

You will often have to make a choice between dividend paying stocks and those that only offer profits with the appreciation of the stock price. Remember that it's always best to play it safe, and in this case, that's investing in dividend paying stocks. While dividends are typically lower than share prices, it's a good hedge against the volatility and unpredictability of the stock market. But you should be careful about stocks that offer unbelievably high dividends. They usually don't last, and you might lose a substantial portion of both your shares and dividends.

Pricing should never be how you determine which stocks to buy or ignore. Also, what is expensive is relative to how much individual investors can afford. For some, a three-figure stock price, especially if the company is properly valued and performs well, is quite fair. Before you go investing, perform your due diligence and make a list of companies that you are confident in. Buy what you can afford and leave the rest.

As much as possible, know the various functions, commands, and terminologies of any trading app that you use. Brokers are constantly trying to outdo their competitors by simplifying the process of trading stocks and offering the latest technology in the industry. This means that you cannot pick any trading app and start placing orders without familiarizing yourself with it.

Thankfully, there are often similarities where it truly counts, and you will likely only need a small percentage of your trading app functions. You should pay close attention to those key functions. For instance, being able to differentiate between market orders and limit orders is a knowledge that will serve you well with any app.

New investors are often told to include business and investment news in their strategy for predicting the market. The issue with this is that some of these investors go on to view the news as infallible. They buy and sell stocks, or change strategies based on the aggregate of the market predictions by their preferred news outlet.

While there is some merit to observing the news, you should take the information received with more than a pinch of salt. Again, it is impossible to time and predict the market with one hundred percent accuracy. There will be a few times when you hit the mark by trading according to the predictions from the news. Most times, you might wish you hadn't. Chapter 5: How to Turn Your Investments Into a Full-Scale Business

This is probably the first time you have been presented with the idea of turning your investments into a legitimate business. This is because the usual structure for stock trading and other types of investment involves one person buying and selling shares and making personal profits or losses. You can, of course, still trade as an individual even after setting up an LLC for your investments, but you also have the opportunity to pool funds with other investors.

Strategies to Expand Your Investment Portfolio and Make Steady Profits

Your successful investment portfolio begins even before you buy shares. It begins in your mind. What are your goals for your portfolio? This question is important because a portfolio can fail, even if it looks like a winner to other people. It should align with your objectives and produce the expected results. For instance, do you want your portfolio to act as another stream of income, or you are hoping for long-term rewards from capital appreciation? Your portfolio should look and behave differently, depending on your goals.

Many of the fees that you pay as a newbie, like the commissions taken by your broker or mutual fund expenses, can be reduced or avoided entirely. And while you shouldn't be motivated by greed as an investor, those tiny percentages that you lose can add up to substantial sums over a period of months or years. To enjoy the compounded rewards after successfully minimizing cost, you might have to rub minds with other investors. This is another reason why networking is a crucial part of life as an investor.

You can try to time the market. This is a highly risky strategy, and not advised for any investor. However, there are those who swear by their ability to correctly predict the market more often than not and come away with huge short-term profits. If you understand the very real risks involved and are willing to use this strategy, then there are two things that will increase your chances of success.

The first is that you must devote a significant amount of time—usually, the greater part of each day—studying the market and how it behaves. You might have to study the market with other experienced investors who also use this strategy. This way, you will know when to buy low and sell high. You should also learn financial management strategies. Regardless of how efficient you become at predicting the market, you will certainly lose some trades. Your financial management skills will guarantee that you remain solvent, regardless of your losses.

The more conservative approach is to buy and hold. With this strategy, you must forgo short-term gains in favor of a more certain long-term profit. This is, relatively, the simplest trading strategy. However, the first point in this list comes into play here. HODLing, which is a more recent and succinct term for buying and holding, may not serve as a passive stream of income. With this strategy, you are expected to leave your investment to appreciate over a period of months or years, despite the fear, doubt, and excitement that you hear on the news.

If you are feeling even more adventurous, you can combine both the market timing and HODLing strategies. For instance, there are certain sectors like cryptocurrency, healthcare, and technology that in the past few years have enjoyed fast growth. For the high returns that you might get from investing in these sectors, they are also quite volatile. This means that, especially for short-term investors, the chances of wiping out your entire balance is quite high if you trade in these markets. Your best bet is to identify stocks with aggressive growths, then invest and hold for the long-term rewards.

One strategy used by investors to minimize the risks of trading in volatile sectors is dollar cost averaging (DCA). This strategy completely eliminates the need to rely on such emotions as greed and fear when investing. With DCA, you can spread your investment over a period of time, as opposed to a lump sum purchase of stocks. For instance, you can buy $50 worth of shares every week for a period of 10 weeks, instead of purchasing shares worth $500 outright. In this way, you are unlikely to suffer greatly (or at all) from the price changes that might have occurred in those 10 weeks. Should you employ dollar cost averaging, you are required to keep making purchases, regardless of the price of your chosen stock fluctuates.

This strategy is especially beneficial to new investors because they wouldn't need to worry about identifying peak market points or the best entry periods.

When you're trying to determine the right company to buy into, you should consider applying the principle of CAN SLIM. This methodology, created in the 1950s by *Investor's Business Daily* founder William O'Neil, outlines all the things that a serious investor must look out for in any company before purchasing its shares.

- **C** refers to the *current* quarterly earnings per share (EPS) made by your company of interest. O'Neil proposed that the EPS of any company must be between 18 and 20 to be a viable investment.

- **A** is the *annual* EPS. This methodology insists that unless a company's annual EPS shows a steady growth in profitability in the last five years, investors should avoid that company.

- **N** simply suggests that viable companies must have something *new* going on each year. This could be fresh products, rebranding, managerial changes, and so on.

- **S** posits that companies who foresee a positive financial future will often purchase their own outstanding *shares*. Look for businesses that behave in this way.

- **L** is for companies that are *leaders* in their sectors. While it is true that one would make more money by investing in the underdogs or laggards—the latter is how small businesses are described by O'Neil—and holding until they grow to compete at the top, this is too risky. Leading companies are usually more profitable and stable.

- **I** refers to the *institutional* sponsors that buy stocks in the most stable and profitable companies. These institutions, like banks and mutual funds, have professional investors who are skilled at locating the most viable companies. If institutional sponsors show interest in a company, then you might want to buy those shares too.

- **M** stands for *market* in methodology. The product offered by a company or the decisions of its leaders are not the only factors that dictate its share prices. In fact, the way the market behaves plays a more significant role in how and when stocks rise and fall. Also, the general market affects different companies in unique ways. As such, it is important that you figure out how things like consumer behavior, extreme climate conditions, and government policies can affect a company's stock.

Diversification is a necessity for investors. Even with blue chip stocks that are typically not volatile and offer consistently high dividends, it would still be imprudent to only invest in one of such companies. In fact, you shouldn't invest in a single sector or companies that are located in the same region. Spread out your investments to soften the blow of a loss. Should an 'act of God' or poor management cause a particular company, industry, or business within a region to fail, you can look to other investments in your portfolio to stay afloat.

The Importance of LLCs for Investors

To truly appreciate the benefit of this idea, we must start by defining what an LLC is.

What Is an LLC?

A limited liability company, or LLC, is a provision for businesses in the United States that combines some of the qualities of a corporation and partnership to present business people and investors with some unique opportunities.

Even though an LLC is specific to America, it doesn't place restrictions on who can own one. It's available to individuals, groups of people, corporations (excluding financial institutions like insurance companies and banks), and foreigners.

LLCs offer similar benefits to corporations, but the fact that it can be owned by individuals and partnerships takes it steps further. For instance, the members (this is what the owners of LLCs are called) could agree not to pay federal taxes on their business. In this case, the members have chosen to identify as a partnership, rather than a corporation. As such, they would have to file Form 1065, which is the Return of Partnership Income in the United States. Each member will be required to pay personal taxes, with regards to the percentage split of the partnership, on the financial performance of the business. This is called flow-through taxation, and typical corporations do not have the opportunity to utilize this feature.

If the members agree that their LLC should be treated by the IRS as a corporation, then they will be required to file Form 112o: U.S. Corporation Income Tax Return. Of course, this should come after they have filed Form 8832 to be classified as a corporation, assuming the LLC had previously been treated as partnership or entity (for LLCs owned by a single person).

LLCs for Investors

The business structure is perfect for individuals who are pooling funds with other partners to invest. An LLC makes sure that other members of the partnership cannot make decisions that could impact the structure of ownership without the agreement of other partners. For instance, a member will be unable to sell their shares without the approval of other members of the partnership.

Without an LLC to offer structure and protection for investment partners, such agreements would be unlikely to stand the test of time. For instance, some partnerships require that members pay a particular sum periodically. Doing this outside of the umbrella of a limited liability company exposes the partnership to defaulting members who cannot be lawfully punished.

You can also start your own investment company after setting up an LLC. Of course, this would require you to be an expert stock trader and fund manager, which will earn you the trust of other investors.

How to Set Up Your Investment Company

As an investor, finally having the experience and skill that are needed to establish a successful investment company is an achievement that is worth celebrating!

So, you've convinced a group of investors to form an LLC with you, or you've built a network and know how to reach potential investors. But the work doesn't end there. The process of setting up an investment company involves more than visiting regulatory agencies and government offices, submitting the appropriate forms, and signing a bunch of documents—not that any of these are not individually tasking. You would, in fact, have to build a brand. And the work of branding, as you might know, begins with naming your company.

What Is Your Company Name?

When it comes to choosing your brand name, you have to strike a balance between what is typical of your field and unique to your company. For instance, it is unlikely that a law firm would be named

Justice Palace. Even though *justice* is a law-related term, that brand name just doesn't convey professionalism. Names like Purity Law Firm or Sam and Gabe Solicitors are what you would expect.

The same is true for investment companies. While there is nothing stopping you from calling your company whatever you feel like, your brand name should convey professionalism and trustworthiness. So, you could have a name like Ben Guarantee, Ben Afford, Ben Advantage, Ben Assurance, Ben Holdings, Ben Trust, or Ben Investment Company.

You could search for popular investment companies or use business name generators to come up with an eye-catching, memorable, and appropriate name for your company.

Plan Out Your Brand

For your business to succeed and have longevity, it must be perceived by your clients and shareholders as more than just a name and the products it offers. This means that you should spend the greater part of your time and financial resources building a strong brand.

You can imagine branding as the difference between merely saying hello to someone and starting a friendship with them. To effectively brand your company, you might have to learn marketing, how certain colors, shapes, and words affect human behavior, copywriting, and customer relations. Of course, these skills are quite diverse and will require some time to become proficient at all of them. As such, you might have to hire your first employees or freelancers. Organize a team and delegate tasks to each member.

Building A Brand: Mission Statements, Logos, and Evolution

Branding is never finished. It's not a one-time thing. You will constantly have to advertise your business to maintain the right image in the minds of your clients and stakeholders. Also, the world keeps changing, and you must adapt to stay profitable.

You must decide how you want your brand to be perceived. As such, you should begin with your brand identity and image. This is what people will remember and feel about your company whether or not they hear your brand name or see your logo. Detail your strategy to create the right brand identity and image.

Study Your Competitors

This isn't so that you can copy every move they make—although, you should be open to learning from them. In fact, you should research the competition so that your brand can be truly unique. You want to be easily recognizable and loved, so take into account the gaps that your competitors are not filling. For this task to not be unnecessarily difficult, identify no more than your four biggest competitors and focus on them.

Identify and Satisfy Your Demographic

People typically have different needs depending on where they live, their yearly income, age, sex, and level of education. As such, you want to make sure that your brand is satisfying the specific demographics that you are interested in. If, for instance, you want to target middle-aged professionals, then going after middle-aged people in general might result in a waste of time and money. In fact, you should further reduce the target niche with regards to lifestyle and behavior.

Mission Statement and Tagline

Your brand's mission statement is what defines its personality to your audience. It tells your clients and shareholders what your company is most passionate about. Indeed, this is the first way that you cultivate and reach out to your target audience. This is because people often do business with brands that they can relate to. If an individual shares the same general ideology and passion as a brand, then they will be loyal customers. As such, you might want to take your time to decide on the vision and mission of your brand.

Note that your mission statement, while it could be somewhat similar, does not have to be the same as your tagline. Take Amazon Inc. for example. Their tagline or motto is "Work hard. Have fun. Make history." Their mission statement reads, "We strive to offer our customers the lowest possible prices, the best available selection, and the utmost convenience". Their mission statement conveys their values, passion, and doesn't contradict their motto.

However, you could decide to only have a mission statement. Tesla, for instance, doesn't exactly have a tagline. Their mission statement is, "To accelerate the advent of sustainable transport by bringing compelling mass market electric cars to market as soon as possible". This mission statement presents Tesla as an innovative company that cares about clean energy, affordability, and creating the future.

Define Your Brand Voice

People are usually only able to form deep and meaningful relationships with other human beings. As such, they give names and personalities to non-humans to bond with them. This is true for pets, children with their toys, and so on. Your brand will need a relatable personality for your clients and shareholders to form a relationship with it. Defining your mission statement and brand identity are a part of your brand's personality. But you must go a step further by giving it a voice. Your copywriting, especially, must be consistently delivered in your brand's voice. Depending on your industry and target audience, this voice can be conversational, professional, informative, and so on.

Share Your Brand Story

To emotionally connect with your clients and shareholders, you should share your brand story. There are different ways to achieve this. You could post an ad that shows you talking about the sentimental, philanthropic, and passionate reasons you had for starting your business. You could also make a short documentary about this or just share behind-the-scenes clips for your social media pages. This tells your potential investors that money isn't your sole motivation, and if it isn't, then you'll keep persevering even on bad days.

Create Your Logo

It's time to create the more visual aspects of your brand. This means designing a fitting logo and coming up with a tagline. To reiterate one point, you can choose to go without a tagline if this is not only normal in your industry, but you also know that it won't affect your brand's relationship with potential clients. If you decide that a tagline is important, remember that it must be a shorter and more exciting version of your overall mission statement.

Having a logo for your company is a non-negotiable part of the branding process. It might require more skill to create a logo than you have. As such, consider hiring a brand designer to help you with this task. To deliver a logo that correctly represents your brand, they must take into account your brand's color pallet, style, vision, mission, and target demographic.

Your brand should not be limited to your website or business card. In fact, it should be infused into everything that concerns your business. Your logo, colors schemes, and tagline should be on things like letterheads, mugs, t-shirts, brochures, social media accounts, and the likes. If you are giving your best, make sure that everyone who sees it knows that *you* did it. This is another reason why the process of branding is unending.

The Importance of Branding

If you are eager to start your business without putting some effort into the planning and subsequent execution of your brand, consider the following points.

Companies that have built strong brands are usually perceived to be more valuable than others who do not have this quality. The reputation of such companies and the relationship they have built with their clients and shareholders means that they can expand their customer base, successfully scale the business, and increase the price of their products and services. All of these can positively affect your company's value.

Have you ever wondered why some companies in the same industry outsell others, even though the quality of their products and their pricing is generally the same? It might be as a result of brand trust. Potential clients are more likely to choose your brand if it inspires trust. This isn't to say that you should try to win the trust of your clients (investors, in this case) and overwhelm them with fees they hadn't planned for. But their faith in your expertise means that you can always charge what you are worth.

You might have heard the saying that there's nothing new under the sun. There is some truth to it. Say, for instance, you were introducing a relatively new and useful product into the market.

As long as it can fit into an industry (transportation, communication, health care, beauty and cosmetics, entertainment, etc.), then there will be companies offering a similar service to the same market. Your job will be to get the attention of your potential customers and convince them that your company is the better option. To do this, your business must stand out from the crowd. Branding is how companies display their uniqueness and call attention to their solutions.

When people trust and are loyal to your brand, this often progresses to referrals. They would want their friends and family members who are interested in your service to enjoy the same quality that you offer. Marketing in this way is the most effective. In fact, all other marketing strategies might fail or be unsustainable if people don't find your brand to be worthy of referrals.

Without branding, you might find yourself constantly moving your company in new directions as a way to maximize profits. This could include drastic changes like new logos, mission statements, websites, and business models. If, however, you manage to establish a strong brand, what changes you need to make might not be as costly or confusing to your clients and shareholders.

Introducing new ideas, strategies, and products might be more easily accepted by your clients if you already have a unique, consistent, and valuable brand. This isn't just because you've successfully fostered trust with your clients but have also proven your brand is necessary and helpful.

Don't Forget Your Business Plan

Business plans are like maps. Without them, you'll not only be lost as a business person, but also have no way to locate sustenance or shelter. Below are some of the things that should be decided on in an effective business plan. Consider them and think about how disastrous merely 'winging it' could be.

1. Outline the objectives of your company. What are your financial goals for your business in both the short-term and long-term?
2. Describe, in detail, your marketing plan. This includes your marketing budget and the means by which you will spread awareness about your company.
3. Who are your target audience? You should list the various demographics that your marketing and branding will be focused on.

Time to Be Incorporated

This simply means completing the process of making your business and corporate entity. By incorporating your business, your company's assets and equity are separated from your personal assets and those of your investors. The process includes visiting the office of the secretary of state (or the appropriate office in your country) to collect the right applications. You will also have to make a list of your company's shareholders in a document known as articles of incorporation.

The next step will be to submit the articles of incorporation and the application form given to you by the office of the secretary of state. There is usually a fee included in the submission process, and the prices vary depending on the state in which you are located.

Register With the SEC and IARD

No company can successfully come into existence without the knowledge of the Securities and Exchange Commission. This is something you probably know but might forget or leave until the last minute. Registration with the SEC is especially important for finance-specific businesses, like investment companies.

The SEC registration is a federal level requirement. On the state level, your company must be recognized by the IARD. Otherwise known as the Investment Advisor Registration Depository. The IARD is a self-regulatory organization that supervises the actions of its members.

Pay a Visit to the Companies You Will Be Representing

This is a very important part of building your investment company. You should make yourself available at various companies of interest to learn more about them and get materials for your marketing. Since, in a way, you will be representing these companies, you want to be able to answer any questions that your clients might have and convince them to invest. If you must, register with these companies to be an official representative.

Advertise Your Brand

It's safe to say that nothing else matters about a business if only the founder is aware that it exists. You could be offering the best service, have the most client-favorable business model, and own the most eye-catching logo. But unless you decided to run a nonprofit, the end goal of your company would be to positively impact the lives of your clients and make money. None of these goals can be realized without advertisement.

In fact, the various ways that you choose to market your brand should receive a large percentage of your budget. It is when people know about your company that you can build a loyal clientele, make mistakes as a leader, learn from them, and grow.

Marketing Strategies for Your Brand

In general, the idea behind marketing is to place your brand in the best light possible before the eyes of potential clients. However, there are numerous ways to shine a light on your business. You should determine what would work for your unique situation, depending on your industry, brand identity, and brand voice.

Teach Your Audience

This is different from talking down to them or being preachy. The fact is that as a brand, you are expected to be an expert in your industry. This means that compared to the average investor you should possess more useful information and experience with regards to the subjects that are peculiar to your industry. By educating your audience, you demonstrate that you have their best interests at heart, and that you have nothing to hide. After all, if they are as informed as you are, you could be more easily caught in a lie. Additionally, keep in mind that your educational content must be delivered with the same personality and in the same voice as your brand's.

Personalize Your Brand Content

Personalizing includes ads, social media posts, and emails. While this also refers to the kind of language and tone that you use, it goes a lot further than that. Poor timing, for instance, is something that many people complain about when they stumble upon random ads. Who wants to see an ad from an investment company when they are searching for the diagnosis of certain symptoms? They might also not be comfortable with seeing the same ad or different ones from the same company ten times a day. As a business, you should invest in data collection to understand things like the needs, desires, and fears of your demographic and potential clients.

Be Willing to Learn

Even the most respected experts cannot honestly claim to know everything there is and will be to know about their industries. There will always be something new to learn and fresh perspectives waiting to be discovered. This is another aspect of building your business where your money will be well spent. This is to say that you should conduct and share original research. Should you happen on something truly interesting, you would be doing a lot more than adding knowledge to your industry and increasing its value (which is highly rewarding in itself). You might also catch the attention of blogs, popular social media influencers, and the traditional media. They could talk about your discovery, share links to your research, and draw more attention to your business.

Try Guest Blogging

In the event that your research doesn't yield any positive results, you could give guest blogging a try. In fact, guest blogging is a useful and necessary part of growing a brand on its own. To use this method, you allow qualified experts to write articles on your blog about subjects related to your business. If you prefer, you can also feature their article on your social media accounts. This way, even though you are unable to frequently write blog posts or perform fruitful research, you can make useful information available to your potential clients.

Make Use of Social Media

To succeed in today's world, business people must understand that social media is non-negotiable. In fact, you must take it as seriously as you would any other aspect of your business. Social media allows you to reach a vast number of people at once, cultivate a loyal following, and control your brand's narrative. You can, of course, decide not to hop on every available social media platform or hire a manager for your various accounts. The important thing is that you deliver authentic, quality, relevant, frequent, and consistent content.

Whichever way you choose to promote your brand, you should try to understand what factors enhance their effectiveness. With social media pages, you will often hear people talking about algorithms. This is what determines which posts should be favored or relegated. As such, you should learn the 'needs' of the algorithms of your chosen social media.

With blogs, you should be concerned with search engine optimization (SEO). This simply refers to the various factors that help blog posts and other website content rank well on search engines. The most effective way to apply SEO is occasionally updated. You should learn what the latest strategies are and apply them to your blogs.

When you start out as a brand, it is unlikely that people will give your business the kind of attention that it needs to grow. This is because you just don't have the credibility yet or they have never heard of you. You can, in the proverbial sense, kill two birds with one stone by paying influencers to talk about and show your brand to their own audience. Social media influencers have continually proven to be more effective than traditional means of advertisements because they have something special: a community.

An influencer is who they are because they've been able to cultivate a following that is genuinely interested in them as a person and might share their interests and values. When such an individual promotes a business, their audience are likely to trust and support that business. However, you shouldn't choose influencers based solely on how many followers they have. You should consider how many people engage with each of the influencer's posts, if the influencer's audience are your target demographic, and your budget.

You should also create an affiliate marketing model. Depending on your partners and how well your model converts, this strategy can be even more effective than influencer marketing. The biggest incentive for influencers is the fee that they get up front. If your brand has some clout, then the influencer can also benefit from the association.

However, affiliates have a real stake in the companies that they partner with. After all, they get paid based on their ability to successfully promote respective brands. This makes them a powerful asset for any business. If relatively small affiliates are able to make a decent earning from partnering with your brand, then bigger affiliates might consider working with you also.

It's generally agreed that social media has allowed brands to build much closer relationships with their customers than previously possible. What if you could take this a step further? While making videos and educating your audience with explainer content has proven to be widely effective, live streaming allows for a more personal experience. Whether you are teaching your audience or showing them around your establishment, they are able to watch this happen in real time. This usually leads to bigger impressions and even bigger sales.

The Best Investments for Passive Income

After creating your new company and brand, your goal is to work as little as possible and to have your new company and your money do the work for you.

Dividends From Stocks

The process is quite simple: buy shares from high-performing companies that pay dividends, the wait for payday. These dividends are a percentage of the company's annual or quarterly earnings. As straightforward as this is, there are some things to take into consideration before choosing this method for generating passive income.

You should keep in mind that the amount you are paid in dividends is subject to change, depending on things like how well the company performs and economic policies. To enjoy more certainty, you should only buy the shares of a company that has consistently paid dividends to its investors for 25 years or more.

Real Estate

If you love a more hands-on approach to investment, then you will feel right at home (pun intended) buying and selling real properties. Real estate investments have also proven to historically be one of the most enduring, stable, and profitable investment approaches.

There are various ways to earn from the real estate market. You could choose to do it on your own or invest with a Real Estate Investment Trust (REIT). If you choose the former, you would pay for and have one hundred percent ownership of a real property. To make money, you could decide to sell the property at an appreciated value or rent it to tenants.

REITs purchase and manage real estate of various kinds. To do this, they pool funds from different investors and pay out dividends.

Peer to Peer Lending

This system allows investors to not only support small business and ideas, but also earn passively. You would have the opportunity to loan money to both startups and individual borrowers who could use the help. The ROI for crowdfunding or peer to peer lending can go as high as 12%. Unlike real estate, you can try our crowdfunding with as little as $25. Instead of just letting your money sit in a savings account, you can do some good and enjoy much higher interest rates.

Index Funds

This is a confusing subject for many people. Understanding index funds does present some complexities, but it is a worthwhile undertaking. Index funds are praised by some of the world's best investors. So, what are they exactly?

Basically, stock market indexes like the S&P 500 are numbers that are used to monitor the value of a group of stocks. Should the value of those stocks rise or fall, the stock index number will reflect this change.

An index fund is similar to a mutual fund, except that there is no direct involvement by fund managers. The money received from investors who are interested in a particular stock market index will be pooled to purchase the same stocks that are in that index. As such, their pooled investment can be made to imitate the behavior of the stock market index of interest.

For instance, if you were to invest in an index fund that monitors the Dow Jones or the S&P 500, that index fund will usually perform in the same way as these indexes. If you are concerned that you might not beat the market in the short-term, then you're right. This is often the case. However, index funds are typically long-term investments, and they always outperform mutual funds with time. The best thing about index funds is that they are a safe way for anyone, both newbies and experts, to invest.

Chapter 6: Personal Investment Ledger

There are different kinds of traders. Some prefer to rely entirely on their intuition, while others develop a plan and strictly follow a strategy. Although the market can be unpredictable, it often appears to repeat patterns. As such, those investors who substitute emotions for a more planned out approach are, more often than not, winners.

Investment ledgers or trading journals (feel free to call it what you will) is a spreadsheet that allows traders to write down their trading decisions. Depending on your preference, you could decide to use a physical book, or an excel document.

Benefits of Keeping an Investment Ledger

A ledger can help you achieve three things: identify patterns, remember the past, and constantly improve. It might seem cheesy and unnecessary to keep a written record of your actions before, during, and after a particular trading session, but journaling is usually what separates consistently successful traders from those who are just gambling.

Identify Patterns

Good traders are able to look out for patterns in their own actions and the behavior of the market. A journal can help you observe this. For instance, are there ways that you are likely to react that could impact your returns? Does your mood affect your trading decisions? Is a particular stock showing an upward trend?

Remember the Past

Unless you've been endowed with a memory that is strong enough to recall every mood, decision, and result during trading sessions in a day, week, month or year, then a trading journal is unarguably necessary. By remembering the past, you can keep track of your mistakes and all the progress you've made.

Constantly Improve

It can be somewhat difficult to make changes in your trading strategy if you don't have the relevant data to support such an action. Your trading journal can reveal, with numbers, your risk to reward ratio. You can learn which days are the most favorable for certain actions and your best performing strategy. This causes you to grow and become better at trading.

There is no standard way to write a trading journal. It depends on what you hope to gain from it. However, it should allow you to note what you believe are your mistakes. For instance, you could write that you entered or exited a particular trade too early or late. You should also have columns for dates.

It goes without saying that merely knowing the importance of a trading journal and learning how to create one is not enough. You should actually create and use one. It is a necessity for any investor, especially those who are new to trading in the stock market. You could, in fact, view your journal as a loyal companion who is always looking out for you. With it by your side, you will grow quickly as an investor and become not only an expert, but financially free.

Chapter 7: Money Management Tips

If, for example, you were trying to lose weight, dressing up properly for workout sessions and doing the right exercises would be good but insufficient. You also need to learn about and follow a diet that fits your goals. But even eating right will not get you the expected results. Consistency, sacrifice, and a willingness to work hard may seem like exercise buzzwords, but they are crucial to fitness.

With stock trading, there are many factors that guarantee successful investors. For instance, by now you should already know the importance of things like keeping a stock journal, writing a budget, and networking. But all that knowledge could be futile if you do not know how to manage your finances. This chapter will teach you how to organize your money so that you are not wiped out by any trade, and you continue to grow your finances.

You should be able to account for all your spending at the end of each month. Whether the state of your finances is good or not, the fact that you might not be tracking could lead to some problems. Thankfully, we now live in a world where applications are available to make such tasks easier than it used to be. You can use them to track everything from how much you spend daily by trading stock to dining expenses.

You can build a good credit score and avoid the extra fees that come with defaulting simply by paying all your bills before or on time. This includes things like credit card debt as well as your electricity bills. Your commitment to paying bills early will also ingrain a sense of discipline and providence in you.

Save up for every big cash decision. For instance, you should save up to buy a car, and separate that money from your other savings. It could hurt your finances if you have to take from your savings for rent or to go on a vacation. The same is true if you want to invest in the stock market. Plan ahead and save up to meet your individual goals.

You should always keep emergency funds. While you hope for the best outcomes in every situation, you should also consider the possibility that the worst-case scenario could happen. If you are not prepared for such eventualities, you just might not survive.

If you don't think about it enough you could easily assume that all your spending is necessary. But if you want to grow your finances, you should take a closer and honest look at those recurring subscription payments. Do you really have to eat out three times in a week? By seeking out and canceling unnecessary subscriptions, you will have a lot more to spend on other ventures.

If you have not hired the services of a certified public accountant (CPA) or you don't know much about taxes beyond the fact that you are expected to pay them, then you've probably been paying more than you should. Find reputable CPAs and have them go over your taxes. If you fall within a high-income bracket, you could get tax returns for things like donations to charity and childcare.

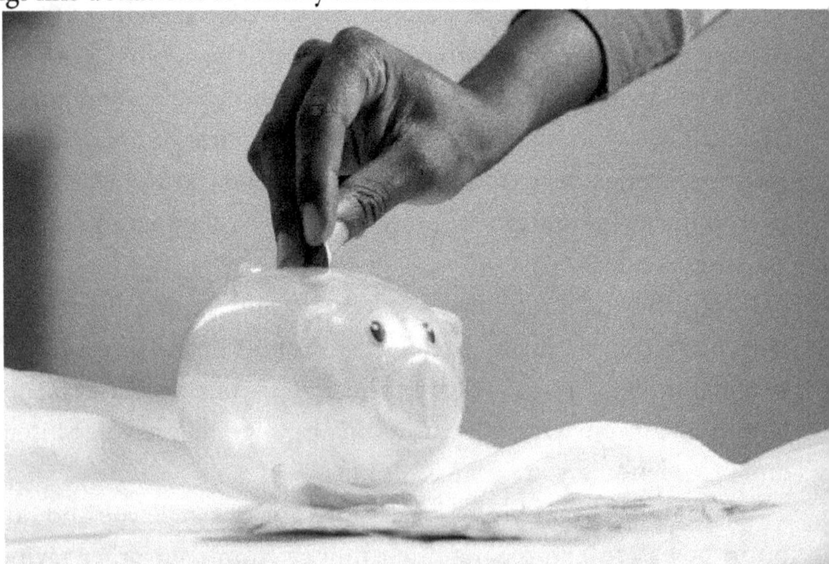

Many people would rather just pay for goods and services without haggling. This, of course, isn't because they don't want lower prices.

Who doesn't love discounts? But it could feel a little stressful to go back and forth with a seller. If seeking a good bargain in this way makes you anxious, then you *should* avoid it. But if you don't mind haggling, then this is a great way to reduce your expenses. This of course depends on where you are doing your shopping.

Seek out discounts. This follows from the last point, but it's important enough to stand on its own. A study found that 1.8 billion people shop online and 63% of all final purchases start online (Mohsin, 2020). Whether you want to download an app that scours the web for discounted prices or wait for Black Friday to make the bulk of your purchases, you can save money by paying less.

The total of your finances can be separated into two categories: liabilities and assets. If your goal is to get wealthier, this means that your assets must outweigh your liabilities. Assets contribute positively to your net worth. Meanwhile, liabilities require constant servicing, which will deplete your net worth. As such, you should figure out which of your possessions (including shares and other investments) fit into either of those categories.

Try this exercise: walk through your house and write a list of the things that you bought on an impulse. You might find that an alarming amount of your purchases weren't well thought out or even needed. Window shopping today isn't just easier but also more addicting. So, you must be careful to only shop for those things that are truly useful to you in some way. If you can, you should allow some time between the moment you find something worth buying and when you make the final purchase.

If you must borrow, then use debt well. If, for example, you are trying to build your credit score by using a credit card for items that you can afford on your own, then you are encouraged to continue doing so. If you have a stable and well-paying job, then taking a mortgage will be less risky for you. But you should stay away from debt if you are entering one merely for pleasure or do not have a sure way of paying back. Being irresponsible with debt can stunt your financial growth and decrease your chances of ever being wealthy.

You might have heard people say that the more money you get, the greater your problems become. There is some truth to this saying, and the reason why it happens is quite simple. As we get richer, we try to make sure that our lifestyle matches our income level. For instance, your biggest expenses at the moment might be your mortgage. But if you get richer, you could decide to buy a car and upgrade your wardrobe. In the long run, these new expenses might make it seem like you haven't made any progress income-wise. You must, as best as you can, resist the lifestyle trap.

Money management is not the same as being cheap. Indeed, you are only encouraged to be frugal with your spending. That being said, you can, from time to time, consider splurging a bit on yourself. This includes treating yourself to a vacation or buying something you've always wanted. If you are happy and content, you'll be less likely to be financially irresponsible. Of course, you should save up specifically to this end. Also, consider investing in gaining knowledge. Save up to buy as many books and courses as you'll need.

Conclusion

If you haven't skipped any chapter before reading this conclusion, then you have every bit of useful knowledge needed to build a successful foundation as a stock market trader. Bold claim, but true nonetheless. At this point, you should be able to provide a thorough definition of what the stock market is. Indeed, you should know exactly what makes the stock market tick and the secret of successful traders.

For a lot of people, stock trading is a cold and complex game that is more risky than profitable. Hopefully, you will agree that this book has shown that becoming a stock trader can be an exciting, wholesome, and positively rewarding venture. You just need to have the right information to enjoy these results as a trader.

As with every other market, stock traders make profits—and, occasionally, losses—by buying and selling things. In this case, stocks are the commodities (of sorts) that are purchased and sold. Most businesses, if done right, will get to the point where their next level of growth surpasses the funds of the founder(s). Even the revenue of the company might be unable to achieve the ambitious and expensive goals that the future success of the business necessitates. One solution to this hurdle is to announce an initial public offering (IPO) and sell shares to interested investors.

Put simply, shares represent a percentage ownership of publicly listed companies. This means that by purchasing a certain amount of shares in a company, you own a proportionate piece of that business. The word stock refers to the total amount of shares offered by any company.

Even if all you had to go on was the explanation of shares and stocks above, you might figure out that you only wanted to invest in financially promising companies. If the amount of shares you purchase means that you own a certain percentage (albeit, quite minuscule in most cases) of that business, then the value of your shares must be tied to the overall value of the company. This is true. Should the company you invest in underperform and lose some of its value, the price of its shares will most likely fall. And your shares will take a hit too.

Ledgers are often overlooked by investors for various reasons, but this book dedicates two separate chapters to this subject. A ledger acts as both a reminder and teacher. You cannot always trust your mind to give you an accurate portrayal of the validity of your decisions. You can lose a trade and, upon reflection, conclude that you entered a particular market at the right time and set your stop-loss and take profit correctly. Instead of chalking up your success and failure to mere luck, you can use a journal to deconstruct the reasons behind your results. This way, you will be more likely to replicate your successes and avoid too many mistakes.

If you also record the date and time that you trade, you can start a daily stock trading routine or know the best times to invest. Even if you are of the opinion that intuitive stock trading is the way to go, a ledger can help to sharpen your intuition by teaching you how the market behaves.

In Chapter 2, we also learned that a ledger is different in style and goal from a budget. While they might share some similarities and are equally important, you mustn't attempt to substitute one for the other. A ledger, as we've seen, tracks your spending *after* it has happened. A budget, however, informs your spending habits *before* it happens. This means that while ledgers record the present and remind you of the past, budgets are focused on future events.

Ledgers are not limited to trading journals. They have, in fact, been in use for a long time. In the same manner that you might keep receipts or monitor your credit card expenses, people used to take little books with them to places like supermarkets and record their purchases. There might be those who still maintain this practice even now. An accurate ledger can be used to write a budget. If you know how and why you spend money the way that you do, then you can write a feasible and effective plan for your future expenses.

We learned in Chapter 3 that there are various investment opportunities in the stock market. While you can have a stake in as many as you want, you are more likely to achieve success if you keep your focus on only a few. We explored, more thoroughly, the concepts of mutual funds, individual stocks, and ETFs. The goal was to assist you in figuring out which of them would be the best fit for you.

To invest in the stock market, you must place your order through brokers. At this time, there are three types: online brokers, traditional advisors, and robo-advisors. They each serve unique purposes that make them invaluable to different investors. For instance, someone could prefer to invest through an online brokerage, as it eliminates human bias. It also offers an almost unparalleled ease of investing, since you can place orders and monitor your portfolio from anywhere.

Traditional advisors continue to exist for the same reason that people still walk into stores today: human interaction. Your decision to invest your money whether short or long-term is no small one. You will be entrusting your money to a system and hoping that it is multiplied. Regardless of how well you have studied that system, chances are that things could go wrong. Dealing with a human being during this process can inspire trust and provide comfort.

Robo-advisors are for the more tech savvy investors who want to cut down on the time it takes to monitor their portfolios. Keep in mind that you won't be able to program your robo-advisor to think like a human being. For instance, it can't react in real time to unforeseen changes in the market or make predictions. However, if you provide your financial statement and investment goals, it can provide financial advice. Your robo-advisor can automatically place orders. As such, you won't need to constantly supervise your portfolio.

Chapter 4 discusses why and how stock traders should form meaningful relationships with other seasoned investors. While it is possible to invest without the support and advice of more experienced traders, you will greatly limit how fast and far you can grow. Even experienced and successful investors continue to expand their network. They do this because it is unlikely that their predictions and actions will be completely accurate. As such, you want to be in a group that can help you separate your good ideas from your bad ones.

Your network of investors can also provide emotional support when the chips are down. More than most people in your life, the investors that you have formed a relationship with will be able to relate to your failures in the stock market. After all, no truly time-tested stock trader has an unbeaten streak of wins.

Knowing the importance of creating and expanding a network of investors, we proceeded to learn how to find the right contacts. Chapter 4 revealed that finding the right people is just as important as where you find them. For instance, you only want to connect with investors who you can form a bond with and learn from, but such people might find it off-putting if you accost them at an airport with your business card.

Instead, consider going to networking events. Anyone who attends such a gathering understands that its purpose is for individuals to form a rapport and exchange contacts. Getting referrals from your friends and family members will also increase your chances of not only making connections but landing the right ones. Social media has also proven to be a useful platform upon which you can grow a personal or business brand. It allows you to display your interests, intelligence, and abilities before a large number of people. As such, it's a great tool for connecting with the right investors.

Now, the fact that you have your personal network of investors is not an excuse to ignore your individual pursuit of knowledge. While you are encouraged to learn from other people, you should expect that they will want to learn from you also. Regardless of how successful your network is, you should be able to prove your worth to your colleagues. This allows for relationships that are founded on mutual respect.

You can expand your knowledge by paying for courses. Instead of worrying about the price of any course, your focus should be on the qualifications of the teacher or course organizer, and how useful the course has been for other people. If there are reviews, read them well. Usually, the best online courses are either taught by qualified teachers on that subject or some of the most successful professionals in that field. This means that the knowledge gained will often make the price worth it.

Further into this book, we saw how investments could be made into actual companies. We discussed the importance of registering an LLC and how to go about it. Then, we outlined the process of brand building. Companies without an established brand will always perform poorly compared to those businesses that are well branded. We saw how branding is more than just a nice-looking logo or catchphrase. They can, in fact, be used to foster trust with your customers and build long-term patronage.

The goal of Chapter 5 was to simplify the process of starting a business and building a brand. It discussed some crucial topics like how to choose a good business name, how to come up with a mission statement and tagline, and what your brand story should be. You also learned how to write a business plan and the right steps to incorporate your company.

Since no business truly exists until potential clients are aware of it, Chapter 5 also discussed some effective marketing strategies. The way you choose to advertise your business should achieve two things; it should grab the right attention and retain it. As such, your style of communication might be more important to your marketing than the platform you choose. Whichever way you go about it, make sure that you place the needs and interests of your target audience at the forefront of your marketing strategy.

Finally, we took a second look at stock ledgers. This time, however, we favored a practical approach. After a quick summary on what makes a good trading journal, we drew up a sample. These days, tools like Google Spreadsheets and Excel are used to create trading ledgers. This is because they allow for quick calculations, but it is not impossible or ill-advised to follow a more manual approach. In that case, the investment ledger in this book will come in quite handy.

The main goal of ***Stock Trading Ledger*** is to get more people interested in stock trading and prepare them for their journey as investors. If it accomplishes both to any degree, then it succeeded.

If you enjoyed reading this book, please leave a review.

References

4 types of stock to consider. (2016, December 25). Nasdaq. https://www.nasdaq.com/articles/4-types-stocks-consider-2016-12-25

All images have been sourced from https://pexels.com

Chen, J. (2021, April 15). Investing: an introduction. Investopedia. https://www.investopedia.com/articles/basics/11/3-s-simple-investing.asp

Cussen, M. P. (2021, March 12). 7 simple strategies for growing your portfolio. Investopedia. https://www.investopedia.com/articles/basics/13/portfolio-growth-strategies.asp

Dillingham, S. (2019, March 29). Here's how to build a strong investing network to support you. Canadian Real Estate Network. https://canadianrealestatenetwork.com/heres-how-to-build-a-strong-investing-network-to-support-you/

Hayes, A. (2020, July 13). How does the stock market work? Investopedia. https://www.investopedia.com/articles/investing/082614/how-stock-market-works.asp

Maranjian, S. (2014, August 14). Warren Buffett doesn't like to diversify - - but he thinks you should. The Motley Fool. https://www.google.com/amp/s/www.fool.com/amp/investing/etf/2014/08/14/warren-buffett-doesnt-like-to-diversify-but-thinks.aspx

Mohsin, M. (2020, March 23). 10 online shopping statistics you need to know in 2021. Oberlo. https://ng.oberlo.com/blog/online-shopping-statistics

O'Shea, A. & Davis, C. (2021, May 3). What is the stock market and how does it work? NerdWallet. https://www.nerdwallet.com/article/investing/what-is-the-stock-market

Perez, K. (2021, May 2). Investment trackers: ways to monitor your portfolio. Investorjunkie. https://investorjunkie.com/investing/how-to-track-your-investments/

Raiyat, M. (2021, February 23). Trading Journal Excel Guide. Logikfx. https://www.nasdaq.com/articles/4-types-stocks-consider-2016-12-25

Snyder, B. (2017, May 1). 7 insights from legendary investor Warren Buffett. CNBC. https://www.cnbc.com/amp/2017/05/01/7-insights-from-legendary-investor-warren-buffett.html

Tashakova, O. (2018, June 6). How networking can increase your business net worth. Entrepreneur. https://www.entrepreneur.com/article/314496

Trader, F. (2020, July 17). The 3 most powerful friends in trading. Collinseow. https://www.collinseow.com/the-3-most-powerful-friends-in-trading/

Zucchi, K. (2020, June 9). 4 common active trading strategies. Investopedia. https://www.investopedia.com/articles/active-trading/11/four-types-of-active-traders.asp

Zweig, J. (2013, February 15). Value stocks are hot—but most investors will burn out. WSJ. https://www.wsj.com/articles/SB10001424127887324432004578306153331261978

www.ingramcontent.com/pod-product-compliance
Lightning Source LLC
LaVergne TN
LVHW022057200926
848481LV00003B/952